# THE ORIGINS
# OF NAZI
# VIOLENCE

# THE ORIGINS
# OF NAZI
# VIOLENCE

ENZO TRAVERSO

TRANSLATED BY JANET LLOYD

**THE NEW PRESS**

NEW YORK
LONDON

Originally published as *La Violence nazie: une généalogie européenne* by
La Fabrique Éditions, 2002
Published in the United States by The New Press, New York, 2003
Distributed by W. W. Norton & Company, Inc., New York

LIBRARY OF CONGRESS CATALOGING-IN-PUBLICATION DATA
Traverso, Enzo.
    [Violence nazie. English]
    The origins of Nazi violence / by Enzo Traverso ; translated
by Janet Lloyd.
        p. cm.
    Includes bibliographical references and index.
    ISBN 1–56584–788–1 (hc.)
        1. National socialism.    2. Political violence—Germany—His-
tory—20th century.    3. Political violence—Europe—History—
20th century.    4. National socialism—Europe.    5. Terrorism—
Germany—History—20th century.    6. Ideology—Germany—
History—20th century.    7. Racism—Germany—History—20th
century.    8. Holocaust, Jewish (1939–1945)—Causes.    I. Title.
    DD256.5.T6813 2003
    940.53'1811—dc21                                    2002040998

The New Press was established in 1990 as a not-for-profit alternative to
the large, commercial publishing houses currently dominating the
book publishing industry. The New Press operates in the public interest rather than for private gain, and is committed to publishing, in in-
novative ways, works of educational, cultural, and community value
that are often deemed insufficiently profitable.

The New Press
38 Greene Street, 4th floor
New York, NY 10013
www.thenewpress.com

In the United Kingdom:
6 Salem Road
London W2 4BU

*Composition by dix!*

Printed in the United States of America

10  9  8  7  6  5  4  3  2  1

# CONTENTS

# FOREWORD

As is often the case, this book began as a short essay that grew as the months passed. It is a summary of research that I had the opportunity to discuss within the framework of a number of seminars, conferences, and colloquia in a variety of countries. I should like to thank all the friends and colleagues who were patient enough to read the text in its successive versions, and then to comment upon it: Miguel Abensour, Alain Brossat, Federico Finchelstein, Eric Hazan, Roland Lew, Michael Löwy, Arno J. Mayer, Magali Molinié, Elfi Müller, and Paola Traverso. Their criticisms and sometimes also their disagreements helped me to focus more clearly and to complete this work. Ultimately, however, responsibility for it is mine alone.

# INTRODUCTION

O ver the past twenty years, Nazi violence has invaded our collective memory and our representations of the twentieth century. Because of the place that it occupies in our historical consciousness, Auschwitz, its emblematic topos, has acquired a prominence comparable to that of the fall of the Roman Empire, the Reformation, or the French Revolution, although from the point of view of the diachronic unfolding of the past, it is not possible to confer upon it a significance analogous to that of those temporal caesuras. The fall of the Roman Empire marked the end of antiquity. The Reformation altered the relationship between God and humans by laying the foundations for the secularization of their ways of life and their vision of the world. As for the French Revolution, it upset the relations between individuals and the authorities in power by changing the former from subjects into citizens. Those events have taken on the dimension of major historical turning points that stand out as reference marks in the development of the West. World War II constituted one of the great watersheds of the twentieth century, and the genocide of the Jews took place within that context. Nevertheless, from the point of view of its consequences, that genocide cannot be compared to the turning points mentioned above. Auschwitz did not change the forms of civilization. If the gas chambers are today perceived as a *break in civilization,* it is precisely because they represent a moment that revealed the blind alleys into which civilization had stumbled and that break's destructive potential. Counter-Enlightenment tendencies, combined with industrial and technical progress, a state monopoly over violence, and the rationalization of methods of domination, revealed extermination to be one of the faces of civilization itself. On the other hand, from the point of view of the history of the Jews, in which, in the most tragic way, it definitely constituted the culmination of a European phase, the Shoah—the destruction of Europe's Jews—did represent a radical historical turning point. It has taken the Western world a good thirty years to grasp the measure of that mutilation. Auschwitz, a laceration in the body of Europe that has not, however, altered the framework of its civilization thus constitutes a trauma that is hard to apprehend, for a historical explanation of what happened does not pierce what Primo Levi has called the "black hole" of its understanding. A yawning gap remains in our almost obsessive *recognition* of the violence of the Holocaust, between the central position that it occupies in our mental picture of that turning point in the century, and the void constituted by its rational intelligibility. The problem is frequently circumvented by antinomic approaches to it. Some elevate the genocide of the Jews to the status of a metaphysical entity, a memory that stands outside history, surrounded by the dogma of its normative impenetrability; the writer Elie Wiesel, in particular, is notable for adopting this position. Others settle for a functionalist historicization, which Dan Diner has justifiably described as "a methodological retreat into a description of structures." [1] The great and unquestionable merit of this "historicization," certainly the indispensable bedrock of our knowledge, is to have established the *fact* of the genocide of the Jews of Europe in all its multiple dimensions. But, however indispensable, that factual illumination does not in itself make any sense of it.

A *historically unique* aspect to the Jewish genocide is that it was perpetrated for the specific purpose of a biological remodeling of the human race. It was conceived not instrumentally as a means to an end but as an end in itself. Hannah Arendt seized upon that point in her essay "Eichmann in Jerusalem" when she stressed that the Nazis assumed the right "to decide who should and who should not inhabit the world."[2] That was an extreme decision and as Saul Friedländer remarks, one that "was reached only once in modern history: by the Nazis."[3] One response to the assertion of the Holocaust's historical uniqueness might be that all historical events are historically unique. But according to Jürgen Habermas, the uniqueness of the Shoah also possesses a new *anthropological* dimension in which he discerns "the signature of the whole period" *(Auschwitz zur Signatur eines ganzen Zeitalters)*. At the time of the "historians' quarrel *(Historikerstreit)*" in Germany in the 1980s, he wrote:

> Something happened there that until then nobody would have believed possible. A deep sphere of solidarity between all those who possessed a human face was affected. Despite all that world history has witnessed in the way of crude bestiality, up until that moment people had unquestioningly accepted that the integrity of that deep sphere had remained intact. And since that moment, a link has been broken, a link of naïveté from which traditions confidently used to draw their authority and which in general fostered historical continuities. Auschwitz changed the conditions that allowed the historical tissues of life to perpetuate themselves spontaneously—and it was not only in Germany that it did so.[4]

Auschwitz introduced the word "genocide" into our vocabulary. The uniqueness of Auschwitz perhaps lies above all in the fact that only after what happened there did we realize that in fact genocide tears apart the historical tissue that betokens a primary solidarity underlying human relations, which allows human beings to recognize one another as fellow humans despite their hostilities, their clashes, and their wars. Recognition of this uniqueness of Auschwitz was a long time in coming, both for our historical consciousness and for the historiography of Nazism, but it eventually brought to an end a long period of indifference, concealment, and repression. Its consequences were twofold: on the one hand, the considerable progress made by historiography; on the other, a collective anamnesis—recovery of memory—on the part of the Western world. But those changes took place back in the nineteen-eighties (they may be dated, symbolically, to the period of the German *Historikerstreit*); their repeated ritual reaffirmation is today in danger of turning into purely rhetorical discourse whose effect is to impoverish and limit our epistemological horizon. Unique though Nazism was, its history cannot be understood exclusively as a phenomenon occuring only within the geographical frontiers of Germany and the temporal frontiers of the twentieth century. In order to study it, it is necessary to adopt a perspective both diachronic and comparative. In the past, the Jewish genocide was relegated to a brief footnote in books on World War II; now, however, its "unprecedented" and "absolutely unique" character is emphasized, and the danger is that this may thwart attempts to apprehend the event within the framework of European history as a whole. Arno J. Mayer is right to criticize the methodology of Fernand Braudel and to stress that Treblinka and Auschwitz force historians to reconsider the importance of *short-term* phenomena,[5] for in the space of three and a half years, between 1941 and the end of 1944, Nazism wiped out a community that had been part of the history of Europe for two thousand years. In some places, such as Poland, where the Jewish community's existence had constituted a social, economic, and cultural element of the greatest importance in the life of the country as a whole, this community was almost totally eradicated. It is quite true that this sudden and irreversible annihilation calls into question the Braudelian approach to history, which reduces events to "surface agitation"—merely a superficial and ephemeral "froth that the tides produce on their powerful swell."[6] But it also underlines the need to study the *long-term* historical premises that foreshadowed the Shoah.[7] In other words, all attempts to understand the judeocide must take into account both the singularity of the event and its inscription in the long view of history.

It would clearly be impossible to apply to the Final Solution de Tocqueville's famous remarks concerning the historical break begun in 1789: "The Revolution, in a feverish and convulsive effort, without transition, without precautions, without regard for anything, finished off what would have been done anyway, little by little, in the long run. This was its effect."[8] The Shoah reversed a tendency believed at the time to be irreversible, a tendency leading to the closure of ghettos, the emancipation of the Jews, and their integration and cultural assimilation into the social mainstream of European nations. The Final Solution represented a historical "caesura"—a break—that instead of speeding up a process that "would gradually have been completed of its own accord" destroyed the apparently lasting achievements of the movement of emancipation that began during the Enlightenment and was subsequently realized in most of Europe in the course of the nineteenth century. But historical breaks, even the most violent and traumatic of them, always have origins. To grasp the origins of the Jewish genocide, we must overcome the limitations that often confine its interpretation and seek its material and cultural preconditions within a wider context than that of the history of anti-Semitism.

"It was the French Revolution that invented the Enlighten-

ment," Roger Chartier has declared in brilliantly elliptical fashion.[9] Similarly, you could say that it was Auschwitz that "invented" anti-Semitism, by conferring the appearance of a
coherent, cumulative, and linear process upon a body of discourse and practices that, before Nazism, had been perceived in
the various European countries as discordant, heterogeneous,
and in many cases decidedly archaic. Anti-Semitism certainly
did not dominate the historical scene. It undeniably had a place
in the history of the nineteenth century, but it became increas-
ingly eroded and forced onto the defensive. In particular
among the assimilated Jews of the Western world, the tendency
was to regard the hostility directed toward them as tenacious
but on the whole anachronistic prejudice—witness the reception of the Dreyfus affair outside France. The birth of modern
anti-Semitism—the transformation of the age-old exclusion on
religious grounds into racial hatred affirmed in the name of science—attracted minimal attention from contemporaries or indeed went completely unnoticed.

The cultural origins of Nazism cannot be reduced to
counter-Enlightenment feeling, to *völkisch* ideology and racial
anti-Semitism. They reach much further. The present study,
which aims to explore the material conditions and mental
frameworks that made the Jewish genocide possible, will have
to go back to before 1914 and range beyond the frontiers of
Germany. Two dangers must be avoided like Scylla and
Charybdis: on the one hand a *dissolution* of this crime in a long
historical process, which has the effect of effacing its particular
features; on the other, an exclusively "Shoah-centric" interpretation of history. The possible danger of a historicization of National Socialism that reduces its crimes to one particular
moment in World War II, if not to a marginal aspect of it, is
clearly that it may relativize the Jewish genocide, or even trivi-
alize it (and that is a danger inherent in Eric Hobsbawm's oth-
erwise admirable picture of the twentieth century).[10] In the

mid-eighties, Martin Broszat pleaded for a "change of optics," which would make it possible to end the "insularization" of the Hitlerian period and simultaneously avoid interpreting the past through the prism of Auschwitz. But this approach was likewise unable to avoid the dangers of a relativizing historicization.[11] The tendency to interpret the Final Solution as a product, neither foreseen nor calculated, of a "cumulative radicalization" of the Hitlerian regime in the course of the war (as does Hans Mommsen, the leader of the functionalist school) reveals the dead ends of a historicization of Nazism that reduces its principal crime to the level of an event without a subject.[12] But to focus exclusively on the criminal, genocidal outcome of Nazism is to make the mistake of adopting an extremely restrictive, even ahistorical, approach according to which the German past is either isolated and criminalized as a whole (as by Daniel J. Goldhagen), or else annulled by the unexpected and brutal eruption of Hitlerian violence. This would be tantamount to either reducing the German past to an anteroom of Auschwitz or else to interpreting the Jewish genocide as a cataclysm without antecedents or causes, as if the mental frameworks of the executioners, their practices, means of action, and ideology belonged neither to their age nor to their civilized context, namely that of the Europe or the Western world of the first half of the twentieth century. Auschwitz would thus remain a total enigma, irreducible to all attempts at historicization, in short, "a no-man's land for comprehension."[13]

The public use of the history that takes shape in this intellectual landscape, which oscillates uncertainly between a Shoah that is blindingly visible and one that is beyond comprehension, cannot fail to raise questions. Paradoxically, the implantation of Auschwitz at the heart of Western memory coincides with a repression, as alarming as it is dangerous, of the European roots of National Socialism. Among many historians today there is a widespread tendency to eject the Nazi crimes from the trajectory of the Western world. I shall limit myself to an examination of the three best-known interpretations of Nazism produced during the past two decades. Not one of them is really new, but all have been formulated in new ways: (1) Nazism as an anti-Bolshevist reaction (Ernst Nolte);[14] (2) Nazism as a rejection of liberalism, symmetrical to Communism (F. Furet);[15] (3) Nazism as a German pathology (Daniel J. Goldhagen).[16]

In Ernst Nolte's analysis, the genocide of the Jews is presented as the extreme outcome of a "European civil war" whose beginning he dates not to 1914, when the old continental order established in Vienna a century earlier burst apart, but to 1917 and the Russian Revolution, which led to the founding, two years later, of the Comintern, a "world civil-war party."[17] This is the well-known thesis that ignited the *Historikerstreit*, debate among German historians in 1986: Auschwitz was seen as a "copy"—certainly a radical and outrageous, even "unique," one—derived from the Asiatic barbarity originally introduced into the West by Bolshevism. What can be the explanation for the Nazi crimes perpetrated by a regime produced by a modern, civilized European nation? According to Nolte the answer is provided by the trauma provoked in Germany by the October Revolution. He claims that Bolshevism—the first example of a totalitarian regime that, right from the start of the Russian civil war, practiced a policy of terror and "class extermination"—acted upon the German imaginary both as a "repellent" *(Schreckbild)* and as a "model" *(Vorbild)*.[18] As he sees it, Nazi anti-Semitism was simply a particular kind of anti-Bolshevism and the Jewish genocide "an inverted—but every bit as tendentious—image of the extermination of a world class by the Bolsheviks."[19] In support of his thesis, Nolte points to an undeniable fact: the massive presence of Jews in the Russian and international Communist movement. Given that the Jews were held to be responsible for the massacres perpetrated by Bolshevism (the destruction of the bourgeoisie), the conclusion reached was that "it was necessary, by way of reprisals and for preventative reasons, to exterminate [them]."[20] Auschwitz was thus explained by the "class genocide" *(Klassenmord)* of the Bolsheviks, "the logical and factual precedent" for the Nazi crimes.[21] So much has already been written on Nolte's theses—both their outrageous simplifications of the historical process, which completely annul the German origins of National Socialism, and also their overtly apologetic aims—that no more now needs to be said.

To be sure, Nolte does seize upon one essential aspect of National Socialism: its counterrevolutionary nature as a movement born in reaction against the Russian Revolution, against Marxism, and against militant Communism. That is true of Fascism, of Mussolini before Hitler, and more generally of the counterrevolution that is always inextricably, "symbiotically" linked with revolution. October 1917 shocked the European bourgeoisie no doubt as deeply as 1789 and its aftermath affected the aristocracy. The alarm and fear provoked among the ruling classes by the Communist dictatorship and also, in central Europe, by the ephemeral revolutionary experiments that followed it—ranging from the Spartakist revolt in Berlin to the soviet republics of 1919 in Bavaria and Hungary—were certainly considerable. But, contrary to what Nolte suggests, the fact that National Socialism first took off as an anti-Communist movement does not mean that its anti-Semitism was born along with the counterrevolution, let alone that it is justifiable to represent it as a copy of Bolshevism. Nazism's roots were solidly embedded in the tradition of *völkisch* nationalism that for decades had been permeating the various currents of conservative German culture. Hitler became anti-Semitic in Vienna at the beginning of the century, at a time when he could not yet have been influenced by anti-Communism or alarmed by the presence of Jews in the Russian Revolution and the political uprisings of central Europe.[22]

But remembering that anti-Semitism preceded anti-Bolshevism is not enough. The Fascist counterrevolution did not limit itself to "restoring" the old order; it "transcended" the past, taking on a modern dimension aimed at building a new social and political order, and operated as a "revolution against the revolution";[23] hence the revolutionary rhetoric of the Fascists, which was as striking in Italy as it was in Germany. But the content of the counterrevolution also mobilized more ancient elements. Although the Nazi movement took shape under the Weimar Republic, its ideology was nurtured by a complex of elements that already existed before World War I and the Russian Revolution, and that were then radicalized in the context created by the German defeat and the rise of Communism. It was from the German and European culture of the nineteenth century that Nazism inherited its imperialism, its pan-Germanism, its nationalism, its racism, its eugenics, and its anti-Semitism. Anti-Bolshevism was a later addition to these; it exacerbated them, but it did not create them.

Furet's anti-Communism conforms more closely to the dominant *Zeitgeist*. Having used a philosophically and historically questionable identification between classical liberalism and democracy—"the world of the liberal and that of democracy are philosophically identical"—he tried to reduce Fascism and Communism to parenthetical phenomena that cropped up in the ineluctable path of liberal democracy. In *The Passing of an Illusion* he wrote: "The great secret behind the complicity between Bolshevism and Fascism remained the existence of that common enemy which the two opposing doctrines would downplay or exorcize with the idea that it was on its last legs; quite simply democracy."[24] In his correspondence with Nolte,

Furet rightly criticized the vision of Nazism as a simple anti-Bolshevik reaction, and stressed the uniqueness of the Nazi crimes, and this makes his analyses more balanced and more nuanced than those of his German interlocutor. However, from a macrohistorical point of view, it was, as he sees it, anti-liberalism that constituted the essential feature of both Nazism and Communism and that, despite their deadly hostility, placed them on a par in any picture of the century. Furet claims that both "are short-term episodes, framed by that which they sought to destroy. Themselves products of democracy, they were also consigned to the grave by democracy." Emphasizing that "neither Fascism nor Communism turned out to be the ensign of a providential destiny for humanity," [25] Furet implies that such a providential destiny really did exist and was represented by their common enemy and conqueror: liberalism.

That was the classic position of liberal antitotalitarianism. In November 1939, a few months after the outbreak of World War II, an American political analyst, Carlton J. Hayes, commented in a similar vein, but in a more dramatic and inspired style:

> The dictatorial totalitarianism of today is a reaction—nay more, a revolt—against the whole historic civilization of the West. It is a revolt against the moderation and proportion of classical Greece, against the order and legality of ancient Rome, against the righteousness and justice of the Jewish prophets, against the charity and mercy and peace of Christ, against the whole vast cultural heritage of the Christian Church in the Middle Ages and modern times, against the Enlightenment, the reason, and the humanitarianism of the eighteenth century, against the liberal democracy of the nineteenth. It repudiates all these major constituents of our historic civilization and wars to the death on any group that retains affectionate memory of them. [26]

The Austrian ex-Communist Franz Borkenau, who described the USSR as "red Fascism" and Nazi Germany as "brown Bolshevism," was at about the same time representing totalitarianism as a "world revolution" that threatened "all the values that have been handed down from Athens and Jerusalem, through the Rome of the Emperors and the Rome of the Popes, to the Reformation, the age of Enlightenment, and the present age."[27] Although unable to allow themselves the pacific and distant tone of the French Furet, Hayes and Borkenau likewise considered the totalitarian dictatorships to be a recent novelty that they hoped would be ephemeral, adding that they represented no more than "an episode" in the history of Western civilization, now crowned by modern liberalism. Half a century later, Furet confirmed that diagnosis, according to which totalitarianism became a kind of *anti-Western* phenomenon. This view of totalitarianism as an antiliberal parenthesis is curiously close to that already expressed, at the end of the war, by Benedetto Croce, who described it as "an intellectual and moral sickness" of Europe's, a deviation from the natural course of history.[28]

Now let us turn to Goldhagen. His explanation of the Jewish genocide is strictly limited to a single cause. It stemmed from what, by reference to the conflicts of history, could be called a form of *extensive intentionalism:* in his view, the sole and sufficient key to understanding Auschwitz was anti-Semitism, not so much that of Hitler as, above all and essentially, that of the Germans as a whole.[29] For Goldhagen, the roots of the Shoah were to be found not in the historical context of modern Europe but in a structural flaw in German history. In other words, he proposed to analyze it, *in vitro,* as the inevitable result of a German sickness the first symptoms of which had appeared with Luther. This is a new version, simplified and radicalized, of the classic thesis of the *deutscher Sonderweg,* the German "special way." Goldhagen believes that the Jewish genocide was conceived as a "German national project" of which,[30] in the last analysis, Hitler was merely the chief executor: "The Holocaust was the defining aspect of Nazism, but not only of Nazism: it was also the defining feature of German society during the Nazi period."[31] The direct executors—whom he calculates to have numbered 100,000 individuals, possibly even 500,000 or more[32]—acted with the support of the whole of German society, which for several centuries had been haunted by the belief that "the Jews *ought to die.*"[33]

In order to confer an appearance of veracity upon this picture of a modern Germany totally steeped in an "eliminationist" anti-Semitism, Goldhagen is obliged to simplify its past and, above all, not to set it within a European context. This vision of a nation of pogromists quite simply overlooks the fact that at the turn of the century the main German political party, Social Democracy, opposed anti-Semitism and included a very large number of Jews among its members. It also overlooks the steady growth of an extensive socioeconomic and intellectual group of German-speaking Jews in the period stretching from the 1870 unification to the Weimar Republic, a growth that, despite the rise of *völkisch* nationalism, was probably unmatched in the rest of Europe. There is no question of defending the myth of a "Judeo-German symbiosis," but it is important to recognize that the Jews did manage to carve out for themselves a place—admittedly precarious and ill-defined, but nevertheless real—within German society. Simply by casting a glance over the continent as a whole, it is quite clear that at the beginning of the twentieth century Germany looked like a happy island for European Jews when compared to the waves of anti-Semitism unleashed in France by the Dreyfus affair, in Russia by the Tsarist pogroms, in the Ukraine and Bohemia by the trials for ritual murder, and even in the Austria of Karl Lueger, the Christian-Social populist and openly anti-Semitic mayor of Vienna. In Germany, anti-Semitism (which, despite its diffusion as a mental attitude, was held as a conviction by no more than 2 percent of the electorate at the beginning of the century) could not have become the ideology of the Nazi regime without the trauma of World War I and a dislocation of social relations throughout the country.[34] In short, anti-Semitism would not have become the Nazi ideology had it not been for a number of factors: chaotic and divisive social modernization, chronic political instability under the Weimar Republic, a profound and prolonged economic crisis, the rise of aggressive nationalism fueled by the fear of Bolshevism and the threat of a German revolution between 1918 and 1923, and—finally—the longing for a charismatic leader, who eventually materialized in a sinister figure whose popularity, without the historical context, would never have spread beyond a handful of Munich beer cellars.

The brute violence of the SS special units *(Einsatzgruppen)* was not a feature peculiar to National Socialism. Rather, it was an indication of how much National Socialism had in common with plenty of the other lethal ideologies of the terrible twentieth century that condoned massacres, ranging from the mass executions of Armenians in the Ottoman Empire to the ethnic cleansing operations in the former Yugoslavia and the machete slaughtering in Rwanda. Unlike these, however, the Jewish genocide constituted not only an eruption of brute violence but also a killing operation perpetrated "without hatred," thanks to a planned system designed for the production of death on an industrial scale, a mechanical apparatus created by a minority of architects of crime and operated by a mass of executioners—some of them zealous, the rest unthinking—amid the silent indifference of the greater majority of the German population and with the complicity of Europe and a passive world. Therein lies the singularity of the Jewish genocide, and it is an aspect upon which Goldhagen's book does not even touch. Its apology for the West, which is implicit in its thesis of a German pathology, takes on a caricatural form when the author explains, in a footnote, that the sudden disappearance of that visceral and atavistic anti-Semitism in postwar German society was the immediate and miraculous consequence of the Allied occupation: "Essentially, after the war the Germans were re-educated."[35] On the basis of sharper reasoning and with more worthy motives, a fundamentally similar thesis was defended by Jürgen Habermas. In his generous plea for a "constitutional patriotism" opposed to any heritage of a German nation conceived in ethnic terms—*Staatsbürger* (citizen) as opposed to *Stammgenossen* (tribe member)—he too adopted the thesis of the *deutsche Sonderweg,* stressing that it was only "*after*—and through—Auschwitz" that Germany became integrated into the West.[36]

The interpretations advanced by Nolte, Furet, and Goldhagen rest upon and isolate undeniable factors: the Jewish genocide was the extreme outcome of an age-old anti-Semitism that had developed specific traits in Germany; National Socialism was a counterrevolutionary movement fueled by its radical opposition to Bolshevism; and the Final Solution was conceived and put into operation during a crusading war against the USSR; both Communism and Fascism, for different reasons and with different methods, opposed liberalism. All the above three readings are based on real data but project it in a unilateral fashion onto the picture of the age and, by dint of a strictly monocausal interpretation, produce a distorted image. What is more, over and above their differences, they share the same apologetic attitude vis-à-vis the Western world, which is seen either as the healer of a Germany that strayed into its "special way" on its path toward modernity (Goldhager, Habermas), or as the receptacle of a nationalistic tradition that was perfectly legitimate despite its excesses (Nolte), or even as the source of a historically innocent liberal order (Furet).

But Nazism cannot be reduced to a rejection of political

modernity or to a counter-Enlightenment attitude. Nazism's vision of the world also integrated an idea of science and technology that was in no way archaic and that on numerous points harmonized with the culture of liberal nineteenth-century Europe. The Western world, for its part, was not exclusively committed to the general principles of the 1789 Declaration of the Rights of Man and Citizen. It had other faces, too, and it also functioned in accordance with other concepts of the relations between human beings, other concepts of space, and other ways of using rationality and applying technology.

The study that follows therefore stands in opposition to the above three interpretations; it endeavours to draw attention to the deeper roots of Nazism and of its violence and genocide, roots that lie in the history of the West, in the Europe of industrial capitalism, colonialism, imperialism, and the rise of modern science and technology, the Europe of eugenics and social Darwinism—in short, the Europe of the "long" nineteenth century that ended in the battlefields of World War I. The latter was undeniably a moment of rupture, a profound social and psychological upheaval that is currently regarded as the founding act of the twentieth century. Without that break, in which lay the origin of the various forms of Fascism as well as of Communism, the industrial extermination set in operation in the Nazi camps would have been inconceivable.

The eruption of the new century abruptly brought an end to the persistence of forms—both political and, to a large extent, mental—inherited from the Ancien Régime,[37] and this violently precipitated a whole collection of elements that had been accumulating throughout the nineteenth century, ever since the beginning of the Industrial Revolution and the rise of mass society—which, to be sure, experienced a considerable spurt of acceleration from 1870 onward. Many factors form the background to the Great War: advances in industrial production that, on the eve of that war, led to the Ford Motor Company assembly line; the reorganization of territory within the various states as a result of the extension of railway lines and the rationalization of public administration; the scientific innovations and developments that prompted the startling advance in communications technology; the modernization of armies and the completion of the process of colonial conquest and partition in the extra-European world; the formation of new urban bourgeois and petit-bourgeois elites, which limited the still-solid prerogatives of the old aristocratic strata and became the vector of nationalist ideologies; the contamination of racism, anti-Semitism, and traditional forms of exclusion by new scientific paradigms (above all social Darwinism), which brought about an unprecedented synthesis of ideology and science. All these transformations underlay the qualitative leap that the Great War marked in both the development and the perception of violence.[38] They were already established before 1914 and constituted the material and cultural bases of the upheavals that Europe was to experience in the course of the first half of the twentieth century.

The aim of this study is not to discover the "causes" of National Socialism, prompted by the "haunting preoccupation with origins" that, according to Marc Bloch, constituted a sickness among historians, who frequently forgot that "a historical phenomenon cannot be fully explained without a study of its own time."[39] The present genealogy seeks not "causes" in a determinist perspective but rather "origins" in the sense in which Hannah Arendt uses this word—elements that become constitutive in a historical phenomenon only after being condensed and crystallized within it: "An event illuminates its own past, but cannot be deduced from it."[40] So it is not a matter of reconstructing the process of the radicalization of the Nazi regime right up to its final collapse, that is to say the accumulation of factors and the constellation of circumstances that made its crimes possible. Rather, the aim is to seize upon the elements of the civilizational context in which that regime existed, elements that throw light upon it and, retrospectively, can be seen to constitute its "origins." The present study owes a great deal to the intuitions of Hannah Arendt that are set out in *The Origins of Totalitarianism,* intuitions relating to the link between Nazism and the racism and imperialism of the nineteenth century.[41] Those intuitions are here recalled and related to new fields of research that have been opened up during the past few decades. Another important source has been the more recent works of Edward Said, who has shown that in order to understand Western civilization we need to study an underlying, hidden dimension to it: the colonial world, a space of invented and fantasized otherness the image of which was designed to legitimate its own values and forms of domination.[42]

This approach reveals a striking lacuna—or rather, once again, a repression—on the part of Ze'ev Sternhell and George L. Mosse, two of the most prolific of the historians who in the past few years have taken up renewed research into the cultural origins of Fascism and Nazism (their works have clearly left a mark on the present book). Despite the differences in their analyses of Fascism—concerning the impact of its symbolic and aesthetic dimension and the role that World War I played in its genesis—Sternhell and Mosse are in agreement in attributing virtually no importance to the heritage of European imperialism and colonialism in the formation of the ideology, culture, mental world, and practices of Fascism. Sternhell quite rightly underlines the cleavage that biological racism opened up between Italian Fascism and German National Socialism, but at the same time reduces the latter to two distinct variants of the same cultural and ideological wave of reaction against the Enlightenment that developed during the last quarter of the nineteenth century.[43] Mosse seizes upon the premonitory signs of modern racism detectable in the rationalism and early scientific ideas of the eighteenth century and then goes on to study the rise of *völkisch* ideology and anti-Semitism within German culture, producing a superb analysis of its literary, iconographical, and popular manifestations.[44] Remarkably, however, both Sternhell and Mosse ignore the role played by imperialism and colonialism in the "nationalization of the masses" and in the formation of a belligerent, aggressive, in-egalitarian, and antidemocratic nationalism. Neither noted the connection between the emergence of this new nationalism and the imperial practices of liberal Europe, let alone interpreted the instances of colonial violence as the first implementation of the exterminatory potentialities of modern racist discourse. There is no attempt here to blank out the uniqueness of Nazi violence by simply assimilating it to the massacres of colonial-ism. But we do need to recognize that it was perpetrated in the middle of a war of conquest and extermination waged between 1941 and 1945, which was conceived as a colonial war within Europe: a colonial war whose ideology and principles were borrowed largely from those of classic nineteenth-century im-perialism—albeit in conjunction with much more modern, powerful, and murderous means and methods. Although the victims of the Final Solution may have embodied the image of otherness in the Western world, otherness that had been the ob-ject of religious persecution and racial discrimination ever since the Middle Ages, the historical circumstances of their de-struction indicate that that ancient and particular kind of stigmatization had been rethought in the light of the colonial wars and genocides. Nazism brought together and fused two paradigmatic figures: the Jew, the "other" of the Western world, and the subhuman *(Untermensch)*, the "other" of the col-onized world.[45]

My argument will proceed on two levels. On the one hand, I have tried to reconstruct the material premises for the Nazi extermination: the modernization and serialization of the tech-nical means of slaughter during the period between the Industrial Revolution and World War I. The gas chambers and cremation furnaces were the outcome of a long process of dehumanization and of the industrialization of death, one that integrated the instrumental rationality, both productive and administrative, of the modern Western world (factories, bureaucracy, prisons). On the other hand, I have endeavored to study the fabrication of racist and anti-Semitic stereotypes that drew heavily on the glorification of science in the late nineteenth century: first, the rise of a "class racism" that reinterpreted the social conflicts of the industrial world in terms of race and conflated the working classes with the "savages" of the colonial world; then the diffusion of a new interpretation of civilization that was based on eugenicist models; and finally, the emergence of a new image of the Jew, based on the figure of the intellectual, as a metaphor for a sickness in the social body. These two levels, the one material and the other ideological, began to converge during World War I, truly the laboratory of the twentieth century, and were finally synthesized in National Socialism.

# I

# *Discipline,*
# *Punishing, Killing*

## THE GUILLOTINE AND SERIALIZED DEATH

The French Revolution marked a turning point in the metamorphoses of violence in the Western world. I do not intend to put the Enlightenment once more on trial in order—in the wake of Jacob L. Talmon—to locate the roots of totalitarian terror, nor to show that the Revolutionary Tribunal and the war in the Vendée produced the forerunners of modern practices of political extermination. Instead I shall concentrate on the guillotine, perfected from the early eighteenth-century Italian *mannaia,* as the representative of an essential stage in the process of serializing methods of execution. If the execution of Louis XVI symbolized the end of the Ancien Régime, the instrument used, the guillotine, was the harbinger of modernity in the culture and practices of death. A few decades after its introduction the poet Lamartine accurately grasped the anthropological mutation that it implied:

This machine invented in Italy and brought to France through the humanity of a famous doctor by the name of Guillotine, who was a member of the Constituent Assembly, replaced the atrocious and degrading torments that the Revolution wished to abolish. As the constituent legislators saw it, it possessed the added advantage of not shedding one man's blood with the hand and the frequently inaccurate blow of another, but of carrying out the murder with an instrument as soulless and unfeeling as wood and as infallible as iron. At the signal of the executioner, the axe fell automatically. That axe, the weight of which was increased a hundredfold by two weights attached beneath the scaffold, slipped down between two grooves in a movement at once horizontal and perpendicular, like that of a saw, and detached the head from the trunk through the weight of its fall and with lightning speed. In the sensation of death, pain and time were suppressed.[1]

To understand the novelty of the guillotine, we need to remember what capital punishment under the Ancien Régime was like. Joseph de Maistre described this public ritual in an unforgettable page of his *Soirées de Saint-Pétersbourg* (*Saint Petersburg Evenings*). The picture that this Savoyard aristocrat painted of the executioner reflects both horror and admiration, for he set the latter up as a pillar of the traditional order. He described his arrival at the scaffold, the silent, palpitating crowd, the terrorized countenance of the victim, his mouth "gaping like a furnace," his shrieks, his bones snapping under the crusher, the spurting blood that bespattered the pitiless executioner as the horrified spectators looked on. De Maistre expressed a kind of respect for this abject-seeming figure who, however, seemed to him indispensable to society, shunned in horror by his fellows but feared and accepted as the secular arm of authority, of a divine, transcendent order that insisted upon submission and obedience: "God, who is the author of sovereignty, is therefore also the god of punishment." For de Maistre, the executioner took on the features of an "extraordinary creature" who embodied at once "the horror and the bond of human association."[2]

In a remarkable essay devoted to de Maistre, Isaiah Berlin stressed the modernity of his vision of the executioner. It was a far cry from the optimism of the Enlightenment, which postulated a perfectible human race, ready to be shaped by reason and teleologically oriented toward progress. To de Maistre, humanity seemed a despicable and sordid species, always ready to kill, the subject of a history that he preferred to represent as a ceaseless carnage. Berlin comments that although the "facade" of de Maistre's writings is certainly classical, the kernel within it is terribly modern: it is quite simply a vision of a political order founded on terror. The totalitarian regimes of the twentieth century were to set about realizing this vision.[3] The power of de Maistre's oeuvre stems precisely from its mixture of modernity and obscurantism, its visionary premonition of a universe of nihilism—where there was no longer room for the notions of humanity, reason, and progress flourished as banners by the Enlightenment—a nihilism enveloped in a sinister apology for the divine order and absolutism. One century later, when counter-Enlightenment entered into alliance with modern technology, this mixture of archaic mythology and destructive nihilism finally led to Fascism.

However, with the decisive and fatal conjunction of myth and steel, and of the irrationalism of the *völkisch* ideology and the instrumental rationality of industry, the "facade" of de Maistre's argumentation inevitably crumbled. The modernity of his vision of an order based on terror was concealed by a sacralization and heroization of the executioner, which upon close examination can be seen to have been already anachronistic at the time of the *Soirées de Saint-Pétersbourg*. In the French Revolution, the executioner was no longer the absolute master of the punitive ceremony, for he was replaced by the guillotine, the new symbol of sovereignty. The terrifying executioner with his royal ax left the stage, and his role was taken over by a machine alongside which he was no more than an attachment, a technician, a manual worker. The new symbol of democratic justice was a technical device for dispensing death. The former executioner, who as Roger Caillois explains was the counterpart "to the splendor that surrounded the monarch," disappeared along with the latter.[4] The monarch, once the possessor of "two bodies," the eternal body of royalty and the mortal one of his own person,[5] now forfeited not only his head but also the dignity and sacredness of a royal execution.[6] The only privilege left to Louis XVI was the coach in which he was driven to the place of his execution instead of the tumbril usually provided for those condemned to death. His severed head, dripping with blood, was displayed as proof of the normality of his corpse: his death in no way differed from the deaths that had preceded it. His mechanical beheading on the altar of republican equality conferred upon him the status of an ordinary criminal. It is true that under the Terror executions remained public—they were not yet carried out secretly and thus trivialized. The French Revolution represented precisely the moment of rupture in which the old sacrificial system celebrated its triumph one last time before disappearing forever, a moment when the ritualized violence of the past was unleashed within the social body that was on the point of exorcizing it.[7] Behind the spectacular and festive aspect of the deadly scene, the guillotine heralded a turning point: the Industrial Revolution entered the domain of capital punishment. Execution, henceforward mechanized and serialized, would soon cease to be a spectacle, a liturgy of suffering, and would instead become a technical process in the production line of death, a process that was impersonal, efficient, silent, and rapid. The ultimate result of this was the dehumanization of death.[8] Demoted from the human race, men began to be slaughtered as though they were animals.[9] At this point execution ceased to be what it had been under the Ancien Régime, a holocaust, a necessary sacrifice to glorify and legitimate royal sovereignty.

The history of the guillotine provides a paradigmatic reflection of the dialectics of the Enlightenment. At the end of a huge social debate surrounding execution in which the medical body played a role of the first importance, the guillotine was the prize that the Philosophes won in their struggle against the inhumanity of torture. For centuries, monarchies and the Church had expended their efforts on refining the instruments of the torturer in order to increase the suffering of their victims. Because it condensed execution into a single instant, almost eliminating the suffering of those condemned to death, the guillotine was hailed as progress for humanity and reason;[10] an innovation that put an end to the inhumanity of torture and the political violence of the past, and thereby exorcized the spectres of the massacres of Saint Bartholomew's Day forever.[11] At the time, even after the massive executions under the Terror, virtually no-one had any inkling of the future effects of the rationalization and mechanization of the system of execution. The introduction of the guillotine also marked the emancipation of the executioner who, divested of the sinister aura that used to surround him, now obtained the status of citizen and, in 1790, became eligible to vote.[12] Within two generations executioners were transformed into run-of-the-mill state employees. In 1840, the *Gazette des tribuneaux* (*Trials Gazette*) described Monsieur Sanson, executioner under the July Monarchy and the grandson of the last executioner of the Ancien Régime: "The present executioner is very different from his father. When he speaks of his profession and the details surrounding it, he has none of the embarrassment and unease of his predecessor. Convinced of the utility of his duties and the service he provides for society, he no longer considers himself as anything more than an employee obeying orders, and refers to his functions with remarkable equanimity."[13]

Four figures were involved in the success of this new instrument for killing: the doctor anxious to eliminate suffering for his fellow men, the engineer obsessed with technical efficiency, the judge who ruled on the right to live of those condemned, and the executioner resigned to abandoning his regal attributes and to donning the apparel of an ordinary "professional." These four figures were to cover a long distance together. Under the Third Reich, they were to play an irreplaceable role in setting up and running "Operation T4," euthanasia for the mentally ill and "lives unworthy of living" (*lebensunwerte Leben*)—preparing its structures, deciding to proceed with it, carrying it out, and defending it on the legal level when confronted by the relatives of its victims.

The guillotine set in train a process that was to be illustrated, over a century later, by Kafka. The subject of his short story "In the Penal Colony," written in the first few months of World War I, is a machine of both condemnation and execution whose features and technical perfection are described to the visitor by the officer in charge of it.[14] It is true that this strange apparatus midway between the instruments of torture of the Middle Ages and the early industrial machines is still a symbol of sovereignty, for it engraves the law on the body of those condemned, but its conception and the way it functions introduce us into a completely new world. The officer of limited intelligence who is responsible for running it, who is indifferent to the fate of its victims and completely at the service of his machine (*Apparat*), has become a mere manual worker, replaceable at any time. It is the apparatus that does the killing; all its keeper has to do is watch over it. Execution is a technical operation, and the machine's servant is responsible only for its upkeep: the killing takes place *with no subject*. No longer the defender of sovereignty, the executioner no longer symbolizes anything at all, no longer celebrates any public ceremony. He is merely a cog in a murderous process whose instrumental rationality makes it totally unremarkable. The rudimentary nature of the guillotine should not deceive us: it ushered in a new era, the era of serialized death, which was soon to be run by a silent and anonymous army of minor officials of trivialized evil.

Following Walter Benjamin, we could say the guillotine, which truly does represent an anthropological turning point, revealed the abyss of death without an *aura*. It marked the end of death as a spectacle, the end of the performance of the executioner-artist, the end of the unique, sacred representation of terror; and the beginning of the era of modern massacres, when *indirect* execution, accomplished by technical means, eliminated the horror of visible violence and cleared the way for its infinite multiplication (accompanied by, among other things, the removal of ethical responsibility from the executioner, now reduced to a mere handler of machines). In the age of industrial capitalism, the gas chambers were to be the means by which this principle was applied. The transformation of the executioner into the supervisor of a murderous machine implies a reversal of roles, the historical tendency of which was correctly grasped by Günther Anders: machines gained primacy over human beings. Soon even the most cruel and frenetic human violence would no longer be able to rival that of technology. With the technical dehumanization of death, the most inhuman crimes would become "unmanned" crimes.[15]

## PRISON AND THE DISCIPLINING OF BODIES

In the wake of Michel Foucault, numerous historians have analyzed the process by which, in the course of the nineteenth century, the "punitive festival" came to be replaced by secret executions, out of sight of the public, and by the rise of the prison as a place of confinement, a laboratory for developing "techniques for the coercion of individuals" unknown up until then.[16] The principle of confinement was now forced upon Western societies. Alongside the introduction of modern prisons came the creation of institutions of forced labor for "lazy vagabonds," the poor, the marginal, and prostitutes—and, at the time of the Industrial Revolution, even for children. During the first half of the nineteenth century Great Britain built a vast network of "workhouses" in which hundreds of thousands of people were interned. Other changes were also introduced at this time. Barracks, no longer the preserve of an aristocratic military elite, were adapted to the needs of modern armies, the armies of the democratic age, the full power of which had been demonstrated by the mass levying of troops of 1793. Factories, around which new towns were built, sprang up with impressive speed. These prisons, barracks, and factories were all dominated by the same principle of enclosure, the same imposition of discipline upon time and bodies, the same rational division and mechanization of labor, a social hierarchy, and the same submission of bodies to machines. Each of these institutions testified to the degradation of work and bodies that was an inherent feature of capitalism.

First Marx and Engels, then Max Weber likened the discipline of the capitalist factory to that of the army, and workers to soldiers. In the early days of industrial capitalism, the authors of the *Communist Manifesto* noted the new face of this disciplinarian society: "Masses of laborers, crowded into the factory, are organized like soldiers. As privates of the industrial army, they are placed under the command of a perfect hierarchy of officers and sergeants." In the chapter on machines in *Capital,* book 1, Marx goes further. He describes modern factories as places of "a systematic dispossession of the worker's conditions of life" and, quoting the social theorist Charles Fourier (1772–1837), compared them to "mitigated prisons." [18] On the eve of World War I, Weber saw "military discipline . . . as typical of big capitalist enterprises." [19] Considered retrospectively, Jeremy Bentham's scheme for a model prison, the "Panopticon," looks like the forerunner of a new system of social control

and for the disciplining of bodies, conceived as a model of repressive transparency that was valid for society as a whole. In a
note to his "Panopticon," Bentham indicated the many possible
applications of his model, which he considered to be useful for
factories and schools as well as for prisons. His project can be
situated midway between the utilitarian vision of a house of
correction, typical of Protestant countries, and the coercive and
disciplinarian prison of modern industrial society.[20] The
panoptic device was intended to be both a center of production
and also a place for the training of minds and bodies in order to
subjugate them to the new mechanical gods of the capitalist
economy.

This new type of prison was developed during the first
phase of industrial capitalism, when the laboring classes turned
into the "dangerous classes"[21] and penal establishments became
filled with a heterogeneous population made up of social figures refractory to the new disciplinary models—whether
vagabonds or prostitutes, pilferers or drunkards.[22] On the one
hand, resistance to the factory system and the dislocation of
rural communities had considerably broadened the spectrum
of social marginality, "criminality," and consequently the
prison population. On the other hand, the advent of machines
had radically diminished the value of forced labor. In this context, prisons underwent a veritable metamorphosis, marked by
the massive reintroduction of punitive measures and degrading practices. The retributive concept of justice and the utilitarian vision of prisons encouraged by the philosophers of the
Enlightenment now gave way to a vision of prison as a place of
suffering and alienation. The dialectic of this process was already prefigured by the reception given in Europe to a classic
pamphlet by Cesare Beccaria, *On Crimes and Punishments* (*Dei
Delitti e delle pene,* 1764). In this manifesto against torture and
capital punishment Beccaria pleads for the right of the accused
to a fair trial and defends the principle of an *espiatio* (expiation,

atonement) that would redeem those sentenced to prison. However, the debate that the pamphlet prompted in Europe centered above all on the rational exploitation of prison labor. The French mathematician Pierre-Louis Maupertuis and the Piedmontese economist Giambattista Vasco even suggested that detainees should be used as guinea pigs for medical experiments. As Franco Venturi writes, the whole debate on prisons at the end of the eighteenth century was marked by a convergence of the philosophy of the Enlightenment, economic calculations, and "something more alarming, an ancient cruelty that now took on new, more rational forms."[23]

Prisons preserved the authoritarian rationality of factories and barracks but changed their function: prison work was no longer conceived as a source of profit but as a punishment and a method of torture.[24] Detainees were obliged to move huge rocks from place to place, eventually returning them to their original position, or to spend entire days pumping water back to its source. In 1818, William Cubbit constructed a treadmill that, having been tested in the Suffolk prison, served as a model for many other British penal institutions.[25] A French observer, Baron Dupin, had produced an admiring description of these English "penal wheels," recommending their use in his own country. They consisted of a number of cylinders of varying diameter, moved by the prisoners walking inside them for hours on end. According to the calculations of the organizers of the English penal system, truly the precursors of the physiology of labor, this activity corresponded to climbing several thousand meters per day. The system was sometimes applied to productive tasks—such as grinding wheat or spinning cotton—but was more often described simply as a "torture."[26] It was a synthesis of discipline that was both "panoptic" (total control over the detainee) and also "mechanical," forcing submission of the body by the technical constraints of this punitive tool,[27] and it pushed the order of a factory to its logical limits, usually dissociating it from any productive end. The reformer Robert Pearson had elaborated a program designed to use terror to deter the popular classes from crime: "To tame the most savage of animals, we deprive them of sleep, and there is no criminal who does not feel the greatest repugnance for the monotony of a life that allows him little sleep and forces him to respect a timetable laid down in advance. I propose . . . that he sleep on a hard bed rather than in a soft hammock; that he be fed a minimal ration of thick bread and water . . . that he wear coarse, loudly patterned clothing. I have no sympathy with the kind of humanity that panders to the prisoner's noble sentiments by rejecting prison uniform. A uniform is indispensable for reasons of security, to make them distinguishable. To my mind, one of the requirements of a healthy system of penal discipline is that those condemned to prison should wear a uniform."[28] As a consequence of the spread of these repressive measures, a considerable rise in the prison mortality rate became noticeable in all European countries.[29] In an analysis of the conditions in the Clairvaux prison under the July Monarchy, Michelle Perrot had no hesitation in using the expression "quasi-genocide."[30] The prisons of the early nineteenth century, in which the labor was conceived purely for the purpose of persecution and humiliation and usually for no productive end, were the forerunners of the modern concentration camp system. Primo Levi described the labor in Auschwitz as a "mythical and Dantesque torment of body and spirit," the sole purpose of which was to affirm totalitarian dominance. He went on to note that this disciplinarian and punitive concept was the very antithesis of the "creative" work praised by Fascist and Nazi propaganda, a legacy of the bourgeois rhetoric that exalted work as an "ennobling" activity.[31] If the treadmill of the Suffolk prison does have anything in common with the labor of the Nazi camps, it lies in what Primo Levi defined, in *The Drowned and the Saved,* as "widespread, useless violence, as an end in itself, with the sole purpose of creating pain."[32] A number of principles upon which the workhouses of the nineteenth century were based reappear in the concentration camps of the following century: the confined place, the coerced labor, the "useless violence," the military type of discipline, the punishments, the total absence of liberty, the uniform, the exhaustion of bodies, the inhuman living conditions, and the humiliation. In *Capital*, Marx describes the English workhouses as "houses of terror" and considered those reserved for children to be the theaters of "a great massacre of innocents" (*der grosse herodische Kinderraub*).[33]

Of course, to compare those two institutions, stressing their morphological affinity, is not to equate them. Their final aims were substantially different: on the one hand, to train; on the other, to annihilate. The Nazi camps were not simply "harsher" prisons with more highly perfected coercive techniques; they were a new phenomenon serving a different logic. The comparison nevertheless retains a "heuristic value," as Wolfgang Sofsky puts it, to the extent that it "illustrates the transformation of human labor into labor of terror."[34] In other words, the world of the concentration camps presupposes an earlier, preliminary stage, that of the modern prison, which occurred at the time of the Industrial Revolution.

## EXCURSUS ON THE NAZI CONCENTRATION CAMP SYSTEM

After the failure of the blitzkrieg in the East, Germany progressively became a modern slavery-based system, which Franz Neumann has described as a form of "totalitarian monopolistic capitalism,"[35] as it threw a massive force of foreign labor into the war economy. Speer masterminded a rationalization of industrial production based on the forced labor of foreigners. Apart from a minority of anti-Fascist or "asocial" Germans, forced labor (*Zwangsarbeiter*) constituted a heterogeneous army comprising civilians from the occupied countries, prisoners of war, and deportees (both racial and political). In 1944, this foreign labor force numbered more than 7.6 million people (many of them women) and made up roughly one quarter of the industrial working class. At this time inmates of the concentration camps (KZ, *Konzentrationslager*) were also working for German industry. In April 1942 the Nazis decided to place the concentration camps under the direction of the SS's Wirtschafts- und Verwaltungshauptamt (WVHA), the Economic and Administrative Central Office, under Oswald Pohl, assigning it the task of rendering the hitherto purely punitive and disciplinary work of the inmates productive. In the concentration camps, the SS rented out the prisoner-of-war and deportee workforce to a number of German companies (*Konzerne*), which thus had at their disposal a vast supply of forced labor, at very low cost, whenever they needed it. Many large businesses set up their production lines inside the camps, and at the same time concentration camps were mushrooming around industrial sites. In 1944, about half the concentration-camp inmates were working for private industry, and the remainder worked for the Todt Organization, which was responsible for the production of armaments.[36] The top stratum of this army of foreign workers consisted of civilians from the occupied countries in Western Europe (French, Italian, Belgian, Dutch, etc.). Next came the prisoners of war from western Europe. Lower down was the mass of *Untermenschen,* Soviet and Polish prisoners of war, who were heavily exploited and destined for rapid annihilation; at the very bottom was the small minority of deported Jews and Gypsies who had been selected for labor and thus had escaped the gas chambers. The prisoners of war and the political and racial deportees were subjected to conditions of modern slavery that might perhaps be termed a form of biologicalized Taylorism. In accordance with the Taylor paradigm, the workforce was segmented and hierarchized on the basis of the various functions in the production process and, as in slavery, the alienation of the workers was total. Unlike in classical slavery, however, the deportees did not constitute a labor force that was intended to reproduce itself but was supposed to be worked to exhaustion and death, within the framework of a system of veritable *extermination through work*. Finally, in accordance with the Nazi worldview, the division of labor coincided with a racial cleavage that determined the internal hierarchy of this category of slave workers. Superimposed upon the professional stratification of the proletariat that was inherent to industrial capitalism was a racial stratification dictated by the Nazi system of values, which implied a radical rejection of the principle of equality. Nazi biopolitics fused industrial modernity and counter-Enlightenment: this was Taylorism rethought within a capitalism remodeled according to racist principles, once the values of 1798 had been buried.[37]

The entire existence of the Nazi concentration camps was marked by a constant tension between work and extermination. Initially designed as punitive centers, then, during the war, transformed into centers of production, they became de facto centers of extermination through work. This contradiction, linked with the polycratic Nazi system of power, was expressed on the one hand by the totalitarian rationalization of the economy pushed through by Albert Speer and on the other by the racial order elaborated by Himmler. An illustration of this conflict is provided by the ambivalent status of the extermination camps, which were conceived not as places of production but as centers for the extermination of the Jews of Europe, yet which nevertheless remained under the jurisdiction of the WVHA. As for the result of this tension between work and death, we should remember the observations of André Sellier, an ex-deportee and historian of the Dora camp, close to Buchenwald, which was created for the production, in an underground factory, of the famous V-2s with which Hitler intended to bring Great Britain to its knees. Sellier declares that in Dora, the production of corpses "in and for the factory" was always more efficient than the fabrication of V2s.[38]

## FACTORIES AND THE DIVISION OF LABOR

If the guillotine marked the first step toward the serialization of methods of execution, Auschwitz represents its industrial epilogue in the age of Fordist capitalism. But the transition between the two was long drawn out. A number of intermediary stages separate the mechanical chopper used for capital executions in the aftermath of 1789 and the industrialized extermination of millions of human beings. The most important was probably the rationalization of abattoirs, in the second half of the nineteenth century. These had originally been located in town centers, but were now moved further afield (as were cemeteries), in accordance with the prescriptions of a hygiene policy designed to sanitize urban centers. The removal of the abattoirs coincided with a policy of concentration which led to a drastic reduction in their number. The abattoir, a telling symptom of the newfound sensitivity and growing intolerance toward external manifestations of violence, testified to an anthropological mutation that Alain Corbin describes as a transition from the "dionysiac impulses" of traditional slaughtering to the "pasteurized carnage" of the modern age.[39] The transfer of slaughterhouses away from town centers coincided with their rationalization; they now began to function as veritable factories. Examples are provided by the abattoirs of La Villette, in Paris, conceived by Baron Haussmann and inaugurated in 1867, and above all by the new abattoirs of Chicago, which expanded at an impressive rate in the course of just a few decades. Animals were now slaughtered as if on a production line, in a strictly rationalized sequence of procedures: collection in cowsheds, slaughtering, evisceration, waste disposal. Noélie Vialles perceptively seized upon the features of industrial abattage: it is on a massive scale and anonymous, technical, and, ideally, "nonexistent. It has to seem as though it does not happen." Even the term "abattoir," a semantic innovation of the period, was designed to exorcize all images of violence. To use the term "abattoir" was to avoid words such as "butchering" or "slaughtering."[40] In *The Jungle,* a naturalistic novel contemporary with Weber's essay on the Protestant ethic, the American writer Upton Sinclair said of the abattoirs of Chicago: "It was the Great Butcher—it was the spirit of Capitalism made flesh."[41] And Siegfried Kracauer, in his *Theory of Film* (1960), seized upon the analogy between abattoirs and death camps, using a comparison between documentaries on the Nazi camps and a film such as Georges Franju's *Le Sang des bêtes* to underline the remarkable similarity between the methodical nature of the slaughtering machinery and the geometrical organization of the space used.[42] Basically, he pointed out, the Nazi *Lager* (camps) were abattoirs where humans classed as subhuman were killed like animals. The historian Henry Friedlander also stressed that affinity when he described the Nazi extermination camps as "abattoirs for human beings."[43]

We do not know whether Hitler had abattoirs in mind when he decided upon the Final Solution, but the architects and engineers of the Topf company in Erfurt, which designed the cremation furnaces of Auschwitz, must certainly have thought of them. The camps functioned as death factories, removed from the gaze of the public, where the mass production of merchandise was replaced by the industrial production and elimination of corpses. Following Taylorist principles of "scientific management," in order to maximize efficiency the execution system was separated into several stages—concentration, deportation, the seizure of the victims' possessions, the recuperation of certain parts of their bodies, gassing, and incineration of the corpses. The directors of the extermination camps were well aware of their typically industrial structure: an Auschwitz SS doctor accurately described it as working "like a production line" (am laufenden Band).[44] And when questioned by Claude Lanzmann, the ex–SS man Franz Suchomel agreed that "Treblinka was a production line of death, a primitive one, admittedly, but it functioned well."[45]

With its industrial methods of execution, Auschwitz thus presents essential affinities with a factory, as is quite clear from its architecture, with its chimneys and sheds aligned in symmetrical rows and its position at the center of an industrial zone and an important railway junction. Production and extermination were indistinguishable, as if massacre (in the gas chambers of Birkenau) was simply a particular form of production, no different from the manufacture of synthetic rubber for which Buna-Monowitz, Auschwitz III, had been created. In the morning the convoys arrived and discharged their cargo of deported Jews; SS doctors made their selection; once those suitable for work were picked out, the other deportees were stripped of their possessions and sent to the gas chambers; by the evening they had already been incinerated; their clothes, suitcases, spectacles, and so on were sifted and stocked in storage huts, as were certain parts of their bodies, such as hair and gold teeth. In his memoirs, Filip Müller, a member of an Auschwitz Sonderkommando, or "special detachment" (teams of prisoners who did the actual work of burning and disposing of bodies), left a precise description of the way an Auschwitz crematorium functioned:

The long hall of perhaps some 160 square meters in area was full of a cloud of smoke and vapor that caught in one's throat. Two large groups of rectangular furnaces, each with four combustion chambers, stood in the middle of the room. Between the furnaces were the generators in which the fire was lit and fed. Coke brought in wheelbarrows was used to heat the furnaces. Masses of flames escaped into the air through two underground channels that linked the furnaces to the huge chimneys. The violence of the flames and the blaze was such that everything groaned and shook. A number of detainees covered in soot and dripping with sweat would be busy scraping out one of the furnaces to rid it of an incandescent, whitish substance. This had gathered in streaks that had become incrusted on the concrete floor, beneath the furnace grill. As soon as this mass cooled a little, it turned whitish-grey. It was the ashes of men who had still been living a few hours earlier and had departed this world after an atrocious martyrdom that bothered nobody. While the ashes were being scraped from one group of furnaces, the ventilators of the adjacent group were lit and all was made ready for the next delivery. A number of corpses already lay on the bare concrete floor, all around.[46]

As in a Taylorist factory, the distribution of tasks was coordinated with the rationalization of the timing. A team of workers had just a few minutes (the length of time depended on the heat of the furnaces) to incinerate the corpses while a member of the *Sonderkommando*, a "time keeper," ensured that the rhythm was sustained. "While the corpses were being burned," Müller adds, "we would be preparing the next furnace-batch."[47] This picture of work at Auschwitz, something in between the photographs in Lewis Hine's *Men at Work* and Hieronymus Bosch's *Hell*, represents a process that the SS and the technicians of the Topf Organization had spent several months planning and testing.[48]

Although the logic behind the extermination camps was clearly not that of a capitalist firm—since the product was not merchandise but corpses—the same structures and methods as those of a factory were adopted. Günther Anders has observed that the task of the death camps was "to convert men into raw material" (*Rohstoff*), and that this industrial massacre was not carried out like a slaughter of human beings in the traditional sense of the expression, but rather as a "production of corpses."[49] It may be helpful at this point to return to the above-cited analogy with Taylorism, of which, basically, Auschwitz was simply a sinister caricature-like variant. A number of the fundamental principles for "the scientific organization of factories" that had been elaborated by Frederick W. Taylor were strictly applied. These included the workers' total submission to those in command, a strict separation between the organization and the execution of tasks, disqualifications and hierarchization for the workforce, and the segmentation of production into a series of operations controlled solely by those in command.[50] The separation of the worker from the means of production was one of the historical conditions of modern capitalism, but Taylorism over and above this introduced the dissociation of workers from control of the work process, thereby opening up the path for serial production in the Ford mode. In American industry, which became a widely followed example in Europe, after World War I this meant replacing the old skilled working class with "working masses," unskilled and always replaceable. Taylor's ideal worker was an unthinking one, with no intellectual autonomy and capable only of mechanically accomplishing standardized operations—in his own words, "an ox" or an "intelligent gorilla"[51] (a "chimpanzee," as Céline put it in his *Voyage au bout de la nuit*).[52] In short, a dehumanized, alienated being, an automaton. In his "Americanism and Fordism," Antonio Gramsci describes the worker of a factory on the Taylor model as a being in whom the "psychophysical link" that had always determined working conditions and that demanded "a measure of the active participation of intelligence, imagination, and initiative" had been broken.[53] Now, the concept of the *Sonderkommandos,* which were made up of deportees (Jews for the most part), who were responsible for carrying out all the tasks linked with the killing process (undressing the victims; organizing the queues that led to the gas chambers; removing the corpses; recovering gold teeth and hair; sorting glasses, clothes, and shoes; transporting the bodies to the crematoria; incinerating them; and disposing of the ashes) obviously implied the workers' total alienation from the work that they carried out. And that was a notion inherent in the Taylorist paradigm; the extermination-camp *Sonderkommandos* were a sinister epitome of this notion. Primo Levi regarded the concept of the *Sonderkommandos* as "National-Socialism's most demonic crime, . . . an attempt to shift the burden of guilt onto others, specifically the victims, so that they were deprived of even the solace of innocence."[54] It is true that Taylor never imagined quite such "an abyss of viciousness," but those who conceived the gas chambers were certainly familiar with modern methods for the organization of labor and industrial production.

Through an irony of history, the theories of Frederick Taylor, who conceived of the scientific organization of factories as a means of increasing production and superseding the old military way of organizing industrial work, were eventually applied by a totalitarian system and put to serve the end—not production but extermination. In the worlds of Taylor and the anti-Semitic Henry Ford (the German translation of the latter's *International Jew* was a best-seller in Hitler's Germany, where it ran to thirty-seven editions),[55] Nazism found the wherewithal to fuel both its urge to dominate (the animalization of the workers) and its community-oriented aspirations (the union of capital and labor). The dehumanization of workers now targeted the *Untermenschen;* the union of capital and labor was the cornerstone of Aryan *Volksgemeinschaft,* or "community of the folk." In this sense, the members of the *Sonderkommandos* certainly did not embody the ideal worker as promoted by the

Nazi *Weltanschauung,* but did satisfy the latter's destructive urge. Destined to die like all the gassed deportees, the slave laborers personified a new figure created by the camps, one that Jean Améry has called "dehumanized man."[56] Meanwhile, work itself was exalted by Nazism as a creative, spiritual activity, as illustrated by the novelist Ernst Jünger's *Arbeiter (Workers)* and the Ferdinand Staeger painting *Werksoldaten (Factory Soldiers).*[57] The mission of the German worker was to build the thousand-year Reich; he was supposed to herald "the new man." Work, conceived as an act at once aesthetic and creative, "a redemptive" act—in contrast to the occupations of the Jews, which were considered parasitic and mercenary by definition—was the means to achieve this. Institutions such as Kraft Durch Freude (Strength Through Joy) and, within it, Schönheit der Arbeit (Beauty of Work) were designed to mitigate the effects of the rationalization of production by limiting or counterbalancing its more alienating aspects by means of palliative measures such as hot meals, clean workshops, sporting and recreational activities, organized vacations, and so on.[58] In short, the relation of Nazism to Taylorism and Fordism was always marked by a certain ambivalence. Although the principles of both had since World War I been applied to German industry—as elsewhere in Europe—and were admired by Hitler and the Nazi engineers,[59] they were rejected as "anti-German" by the directors of the *Deutsches Institut für Technische Arbeitsschulung* (DINTA), the German Institute for Technical Vocational Training.[60]

## BUREAUCRATIC ADMINISTRATION

Like all business enterprises, a factory that produced death was run by a rational administration based upon the principles of calculation, specialization, and the segmentation of tasks into a series of partial, seemingly independent yet coordinated operations. The agents of this bureaucratic apparatus did not control the process as a whole, and when they did learn of its final purpose they could justify themselves by saying that they had borne no responsibility and were simply obeying orders, or else that their own limited and partial function was in itself in no way criminal.

Max Weber realized that moral indifference constituted an essential feature of modern bureaucracy, which was specialized and therefore irreplaceable, but separated from the means of work and unaffected by the final outcome of its actions. In *Economy and Society* he sketched in the following picture: "When fully developed, bureaucracy also stands, in a specific sense, under the principle of *sine ira ac studio*. Bureaucracy develops the more perfectly the more it is 'dehumanized,' the more completely it succeeds in eliminating from official business [*Amtgeschäfte*] love, hatred, and all purely personal, irrational, and emotional elements which escape calculation. This is appraised as its special virtue by capitalism." Weber goes on to say that the embodiment of this tendency peculiar to the instrumental rationality of the Western world is the "specialist" (*Fachmann*), who is "rigorously objective" and at the same time "indifferent to the affairs of men."[61] Raul Hilberg, the principal historian of the destruction of the Jews of Europe, has described the bureaucracy of the Final Solution in strictly Weberian terms:

> Most bureaucrats composed memoranda, drew up blueprints, signed correspondence, talked on the telephone, and participated in conferences. They could destroy a whole people by sitting at their desks. Except for inspection tours, which were not obligatory, they never had to see "100 bodies lie there, or 500 or 1,000." However, these men were not naïve. They realized the connection between their paper-work and the heaps of corpses in the East, and they also realized the shortcomings

of arguments that placed all evil on the side of the Jew and all good on the German. That was why they were compelled to justify their individual activities.[62]

The justifications that they put forward in the postwar trials simply reaffirmed the well-known principles of the moral world of administrators: they were obeying orders, carrying out duties perceived as a "mission," and so on. In the vast majority of cases, the zeal of these bureaucrats of the Final Solution did not stem from anti-Semitism—not that they were unaffected by it, far from it. Hatred of the Jews was not the motive for their behavior. Their zeal in applying the measures of persecution and in setting up the logistical apparatus of extermination was prompted as much by professional habit as by a generalized indifference.[63] After the war, most of them continued their careers as state employees, managers, and statisticians in West Germany, some even in East Germany.

The bureaucracy thus played a crucial role in the genocide of the Jews of Europe. The extermination process relied on the bureaucracy as its essential organ of transmission and execution. The *wissenschaftliche Soldaten* or "soldiers of science," as the Third Reich dubbed statisticians, neither conceived nor were responsible for Nazi policy, but they were its instrument.[64] It was the bureaucracy that organized the application of the Nuremberg Laws, the census of the Jews and the partial Jews, the expropriation of Jewish property within the framework of measures for the "Aryanization" of the economy, the herding of Jews into ghettos and their subsequent deportation, the management of the concentration camps and the killing centers. This bureaucratic apparatus played an essential role in the implementation of Nazi crimes without ever calling into question the charismatic radicalization of the regime.[65] The mechanism of Nazi decision making underwent major changes during the war, moving from the passing of laws

(Nuremberg, 1935) to the issuing of written but not published directives (recorded by the 1942 Wannsee Conference) and finally to giving oral orders (for setting the gas chambers in operation).[66] But even when it had abandoned the practice of legal formalization, Nazism still needed a modern, efficient, and rational bureaucracy. Once the killing centers were in operation, following the wave of massacres that had accompanied the blitzkrieg in the East, this army of executives welded to their desks became the heart of the system for destroying the Jews. The propaganda and publicity for the first anti-Semitic measures taken against the Jews (the autos-da-fé, the Nuremberg Laws, the Aryanization of the economy, and the pogroms of the Kristallnacht) were replaced by the coded language of the operations of extermination, which was strictly based on administrative jargon, according to which the murder was referred to as the Final Solution (*Endlösung*), the executions were "special treatment" (*Sonderbehandlung*), and the gas chambers were "special installations" (*Spezialeinrichtungen*). The bureaucracy was the instrument of Nazi violence, and that instrument was an authentic product of what must be called the civilizing process (an expression borrowed from Norbert Elias but with conclusions diametrically opposed to his),[67] which included such features as the sociogenesis of the state, administrative rationalization, state monopoly over the means of coercion and violence, and drive controls.[68] That is why Adorno regarded Nazism as the expression of a barbarity "written into the very principle of civilization."

The string of developments that connect Nazism, two centuries later, to the modern prison promoted by Bentham's "Panopticon" and to the guillotine first used during the French Revolution can now be seen in a different light. Nazi violence integrated and developed the paradigms that underlie those two institutions of Western modernity. The paradigm of the guillotine—involving mechanical execution, serialized death, indirect killing, the exoneration of any ethical responsibility on the part of the executioners, slaughtering as a "subjectless" process—triumphed in the technological massacres of the twentieth century. And the paradigm of the prison—with its principle of confinement, dehumanizing the detainees, its regime designed to exhaust and discipline bodies and enforce submission to its hierarchies, and its administrative rationality—ultimately led to the concentration camps of totalitarian regimes. The Nazi extermination camps realized the fusion of those two paradigms, which spawned something appallingly new and historically unprecedented that no longer had very much to do with either capital punishment or penal establishments. Those camps created an industrial system for slaughter in which modern technology, the division of labor, and administrative rationality were all interrelated, as in a business project. The victims of that project were, strictly speaking, no longer "detainees" but simply the "raw material"—dehumanized living beings—necessary for the mass production of corpses. The new and unprecedented threshold crossed by the gas chambers should not obscure the original connection, which reveals the Nazi extermination to be the end result and synthesis of a long historical process that began in the late eighteenth century.

# 2

# *Conquest*

## IMPERIALISM

The rise of industrial civilization was accompanied by the conquest and colonization of Africa. In the European imaginary the two became intertwined. The world of machines, trains, and industrial production could not be fully understood by citizens of industrializing nations unless set in opposition to the living portrait of a primitive, savage dark age.[1] In the imperialist world's vision, purveyed by the press and by a rich popular iconography, the dichotomy between civilization and barbarity was given concrete form in the image of an imposing ship manned by Europeans in colonial uniform navigating along huge African rivers, through a landscape of straw huts, naked, black-skinned people, and hippopotami and crocodiles. In literature, Joseph Conrad immortalized the African stereotype: "Going up that river was like traveling back to the earliest beginnings of the world."[2]

The metamorphoses of modern racism are largely indissociable from the process of colonization in Asia and Africa, from the first "scientific" systematizations of Gobineau (1816–1882)—the hierarchization of the human races, and the vision of crossbreeding as a source of degeneration for the superior races and of the decadence of civilization—to the later elaborations of Georges Vacher de Lapouge and Houston Stewart Chamberlain, whose writings were already deeply contaminated by social Darwinism, medical anthropology, eugenics, and racial biology. The racists of the late nineteenth century rejected Gobineau's resignation in the face of the decadence of the West—in which Arendt detected a projection of the decline of the European aristocracy[3]—and recommended new therapies that were to be tried out for the first time in the colonial world, including the "selection" of races and the extermination of conquered peoples, which was represented as the "natural law" of historical development. It was precisely this desire to "regenerate," this aspiration toward a new world order and new relations of domination between people, that marked the transition from an ideology of decadence to vitalism, from an apology for the traditional order to a cult of technical modernity as the source of conquest and power—in other words, that favored the move from conservatism to Fascism. Biological racism and colonialism now surged forward together, bolstered by two complementary types of discourse, one that promoted Europe's "civilizing mission" and the other that encouraged the "extinction" of "inferior races": conquest through extermination.

In 1876, King Leopold II of Belgium produced an inspired panegyric of colonialism in which all the commonplaces of the Eurocentric spirit of the nineteenth century found expression: "To open up to civilization the only part of our globe that it has not yet penetrated, to pierce the darkness that envelops entire populations, that—I dare to claim—is a *crusade* worthy of an age of progress."[4] Carl Schmitt cited this passage in *Der Nomos der Erde,* interpreting it as the crowning ambition of the *jus publicum europaeum* of which international law was simply an extension and which quite naturally authorized wars of conquest outside Europe. Many traces of such a vision of the world are detectable in classic liberalism. John Stuart Mill, who was also a director of the East India Company, explained at the beginning of his famous essay on liberty, "Despotism is a legitimate mode of government in dealing with barbarians."[5] In *Principles of Political Economy,* Mill stressed that the West Indies were not countries in the Western sense of the term, but "the place where England finds it convenient to carry on the production of sugar, coffee, and a few other tropical commodities."[6] Alexis de Tocqueville, who certainly saluted the aristocratic "pride" of the Indian tribes of America and deplored their massacre, nevertheless declared that they "occupied" that continent but did not "possess" it. They lived amid the riches of the New World like temporary residents, as if Providence had afforded them no more than a "short-term use" of it. Tocqueville went on to say that they were simply there "waiting" to be replaced by the Europeans, the legitimate proprietors of the land.[7] In his correspondence he suggested that the westward expansion of the United States was a model for the colonization of Algeria,[8] where "total domination" was the natural goal of the French armies, in comparison to which the destruction of villages and the massacre of their Arab populations were merely "regrettable necessities."[9]

Edward Said and Michael Adas are right to stress that the colonial culture is not just a form of propaganda and that the imperialist ideology should be taken seriously: nineteenth-century Europe was truly convinced that it was accomplishing a civilizing mission in Asia and Africa.[10] At the time of decolonization, the imperialist culture was stigmatized, violently rejected, and subsequently forgotten; it never became the subject of in-depth analysis, and today remains still largely repressed.[11] Yet the intelligibility of the twentieth century would be considerably enhanced if that amnesia lifted, for then the link between National Socialism and classic imperialism would no longer be obscured as it is at present. To several analysts of the thirties and forties, however, it was certainly perfectly clear. Ernst Jünger was reading Joseph Conrad's *Heart of Darkness* as a Wehrmacht officer in Paris in 1942. Contemporary events conferred a definite topicality upon this tale about the colonization of the Congo, which described "the switch from a civilizing optimism to total bestiality." In his diary, Jünger noted that the story's hero had "recognized the strains of the overture to our century."[12] In 1942, Karl Korsch, a German Marxist philosopher then in exile in the United States, attempted a historical interpretation of the violence of the war which called the global dynamic of the West into question: "The novelty of totalitarian politics in this respect is simply that the Nazis have extended to 'civilized' European peoples the methods hitherto reserved for the 'natives' or 'savages' living outside so-called civilization."[13]

In *The Origins of Totalitarianism,* a work published in 1951 but containing several texts written during the war years, Hannah Arendt identified European imperialism as an essential stage in the genesis of Nazism. The episodes of nineteenth-century colonial violence seemed to her to prefigure the crimes that were perpetrated a century later against Europeans, particularly the Jews, who were the victims of a genocide conceived as an operation of racial purging. In part 2 of her book, titled "Imperialism," she described the nineteenth-century policies of colonial domination as the first synthesis between *massacre* and *administration,* a synthesis of which, in her view, the Nazi camps produced the ultimate form. Modern racism (justified in the name of science) and bureaucracy (the most perfect embodiment of Western rationality) originated separately but evolved along parallel lines. They came together in Africa. The conquest of this continent, achieved with modern weaponry and planned by the military and civilian bureaucracy, revealed a hitherto unprecedented potential for violence. Arendt used a striking expression at this point. She wrote of

"administrative massacres" that, it seemed to her, prefigured
the Nazi extermination camps:

> When the European mob discovered what a "lovely virtue" a
> white skin could be in Africa, when the English conqueror in
> India became an administrator who no longer believed in the
> universal validity of law, but was convinced of his own innate
> capacity to rule and dominate, . . . the stage seemed to be set
> for all possible horrors. Lying under anybody's nose were
> many of the elements which, gathered together, could create a
> totalitarian government on the basis of racism. "Administra-
> tive massacres" were proposed by Indian bureaucrats, while
> African officials declared that "no ethical considerations such
> as the rights of man will be allowed to stand in the way" of the
> white rule.[14]

The notion of "living space" was not a Nazi invention. It
was simply the German version of a commonplace of European
culture at the time of imperialism, in the same way as Malthu-
sianism was in Great Britain. The idea of a "living space" inspired a policy of conquest and was invoked to justify the goals
of pan-Germanism. Meanwhile, Malthusian theories were
regularly used to legitimate famine in India—which some
observers of the time accepted as "a salutary cure for over-
population."[15] The concept of "living space," as much as the
"population principle," postulated a hierarchy in the right to
existence, which became the prerogative of the nations, or even
"races," that were dominant. The expression "Lebensraum"
was coined in 1901, under Kaiser Wilhelm, by the German
geographer Friedrich Ratzel (1844–1904) and had become
part of the vocabulary of German nationalism well before the
advent of Nazism. It resulted from the fusion of social Darwinism and imperialist geopolitics, and stemmed from a vision of
the extra-European world as a space to be colonized by biologi-

cally superior groups. For Ratzel, the "living space" was essential in order to reestablish a balance, in Germany, between the industrial development, which was by now irreversible, and agriculture, which was thereby threatened. In their colonies, the Germans would reestablish harmonious relations with nature and preserve their vocation as a people wedded to the land.[16] Under the empire of Kaiser Wilhelm, the idea of *Lebensraum* inspired a current of pan-Germanism and was the basis for a widespread demand for a *Weltpolitik,* international policy, that would assign Germany an international position comparable to that of France and Great Britain. The expectation that this would be brought about by a policy of colonial expansion in the East, in a world populated by *Untermenschen,* was taken for granted by many nationalist Germans as early as the end of the nineteenth century, when the notions of *Mittelafrika* (central Africa) and *Mitteleuropa* (central Europe) started to be associated as two indissociable aspects of German foreign policy. The symptoms of a vision of the world such as this, which attributed "a civilizing mission" in eastern Europe to the Germans, are easily detectable in the work not only of Heinrich von Treitschke but also of the young Max Weber.[17]

The Altdeutscher Verbund (Pan-German League), founded in 1893, was the central dispenser of propaganda for this colonial project. By the end of the nineteenth century, several of its representatives had elaborated plans for a Germanization of the Slavic world, which in some cases implied marginalizing, in others expelling "non-Germanic" populations. Some of these plans—for example those elaborated in the geographer Paul Langhans's *Ein Pangermanistisches Deutschland* (1905)— were linked to legal measures of racist if not eugenic inspiration (prohibiting mixed marriages, enforcing sterilization) that paved the way for the Nuremberg Laws of 1935.[8] During World War I, all the necessary conditions for beginning to apply these pan-German programs seemed to be in place. At

the time of the Treaty of Brest Litovsk in 1918, which official-
ized the modification of the eastern frontiers, the German government had envisaged a policy for the Germanization of the
occupied territories, accompanied by the enforced displace-
ment of some Slav populations.[19] Under the Weimar Republic,
following the amputations inflicted upon Germany by the
Treaty of Versailles, those claims were to be revoiced and radicalized by the National Socialists, who reformulated them in
racist terms in an aggressively imperialistic program.

In the early twenties, the *völkisch* writer Hans Grimm produced a novel titled *Volk ohne Raum* (*A People Without Space*),
which popularized the idea of "living space" and was extremely
successful. In his novel, Grimm, who would join the German
National Socialist Workers Party in 1930, recounted the tale of
Freibott, a German who had traveled to German West Africa
and who, having helped to repress a native revolt, remade his
life far from all industrialized towns, in contact with a still un-
contaminated nature that was a replacement for the German
forests that were already surrounded by factory chimneys and
criss-crossed by motorways. Needless to say, the corollary to
this Germanic paradise in South-West Africa was the strictest
racial segregation. In 1920, the last German governor in Africa,
Heinrich Schnee, organized the production of an ambitious
*Deutsches Koloniallexicon* (*German Colonial Lexicon*) in three
volumes, to which he contributed an article entitled "Verkaf-
ferung" ("Kaffir-ization"), meaning "the regression of Europeans to the cultural level of a native" ("kaffir" being a
disparaging term for a black African). In order to prevent such
degeneration as a result of life in the bush, contact with colored
peoples, and, above all, sexual relations with the indigenous
population—which would inevitably lead to diminished intelligence and lower productivity—Schnee advocated a regime of
racial segregation.[20] The Nuremberg Laws of the Nazis
shocked the Europe of the 1930s because they were directed

against a group, Jews, that had been emancipated for a whole century and that was perfectly well integrated into German society and culture. Yet the entire club of colonial powers had already envisaged such laws as normal and natural measures to be taken with regard to the non-European world. There exists a vast bibliography relating to the history of anti-Semitism in Germany and Hitler's ideological ancestors and theoretical sources of inspiration, ranging from Richard Wagner to Arthur Moeller van den Bruck, and from Wilhelm Marr to Houston Stewart Chamberlain. But very few works attempt to explain the Nazi crimes in the light of both German and more generally European colonial cultures and practices. Emphasis is placed on the specific features of Nazi anti-Semitism but not on its roots in a theory and practice of extermination of "inferior races" to which all the imperial Western powers subscribed.

## THE "EXTINCTION OF RACES"

In the Western culture of the nineteenth century, "colonialism," "a civilizing mission," "the rights of conquest," and practices of "extermination" were frequently virtually synonymous terms. A vast literature—partly scientific and partly popular, made up of scholarly works, anthropological reviews, travelers' tales, and novels and stories aimed at both the educated and the working classes—fostered belief in the principle of the West's right to dominate the world, to colonize the planet, and to subjugate or even eliminate "savage peoples." Where colonization involved the total eradication of native populations, as in the United States, that principle was affirmed most explicitly: in 1850, at the height of the stampede to grab lands in the West, the American anthropologist Robert Knox declared in *The Race of Man* that "extermination" was, quite simply, "a law of Anglo-Saxon America."[21] Such frankness was less frequent among the scholars of Victorian England, who preferred to refer to the matter in terms of "the extinction of inferior races." Around the middle of the nineteenth century, this idea became integrated into European culture as an established fact, which social Darwinism then set out to prove at a scientific level. The ethos of triumphant capitalism was a mixture, in varying proportions, of the ideas of Adam Smith, Thomas Malthus, Charles Darwin, Auguste Comte, and Herbert Spencer—in other words a combination of laissez-faire economics, the population principle, the theory of natural selection, positivist determinism, and evolutionism. It richly deserved the definition that Lukács was to give it: "a pseudo-biological defense of class privileges." [22] One of the great discoveries of this ethos was "the extinction of inferior races," and this was one of its favorite subjects of debate. In 1864 it was the theme of a discussion organized by the London Anthropological Society, in which imperialism was provided with theoretically solid scientific bases, accompanied by a substantial dose of Victorian moralizing. The debate opened with a report from Dr. Richard Lee, who, drawing on the example of New Zealand, remarked upon "the rapid disappearance of aboriginal tribes" in the face of the advance of civilization, from which he concluded that "Europe may have for her destiny to repopulate the globe." [23] Lee explained that the high mortality rate among the Maoris and Polynesians was certainly partly a result of diseases introduced by the Europeans, but claimed that there were deeper causes for the phenomenon. He concluded, "We must regard it as an illustration of the crudest forms of humanity, with certain groups shrinking and passing away before others that are enlightened with intelligence and endowed with intellectual superiority." [24] Thomas Bendyshe, a theorist of the natural selection of races, made a contribution to the discussion in which he cited an American social Darwinist, a Professor Waitz, according to whom we should not simply "acknowledge the right of the White American to destroy the red man but perhaps give him credit for having acted as the instrument of Providence in carrying out and promoting the law of destruction" (note "red man" in lowercase letters and "White American" in upper case).[25] Bendyshe then added some general remarks relating to the American experience: "Some morbid philanthropists, who have formed associations for the preservation of these races, attribute their extinction to the aggression by fire and sword inflicted upon them by the settlers, and the deadly diseases that the latter introduce. Although to some extent this may be the case, it simply confirms the effects of a more powerful law that dictates the inferior race will eventually be swallowed up by the superior."[26] Alfred Russel Wallace, along with Darwin the founder of the idea of natural selection, also contributed to the debate. He reaffirmed the same law of "the preservation of favoured races in the struggle for life," the inevitable consequence of which is "the extinction of all those low and mentally undeveloped populations with which Europeans come into contact."[27] As he saw it, this law explained the disappearance of the Indians in North America and Brazil and of the Tasmanians, Maoris, and other indigenous populations in Australia and New Zealand. He went on to produce a biological justification of imperialism:

> The intellectual and moral, as well as the physical, qualities of the European are superior, the same powers and capacities— which have made him rise in a few centuries from the condition of a wandering savage, with a scanty and stationary population, to his present stage of culture and advancement, with a greater average longevity, a greater average strength, and a capacity of more rapid increase,—enable him, when in contact with the savage man, to conquer in the struggle for existence, and to increase at his expense, just as the better adapted increase at the expense of the less adapted varieties in

the animal and vegetable kingdoms,—just as the weeds of Europe overrun North America and Australia, extinguishing native productions by the inherent vigour of their organization, and by their greater capacity for existence and multiplication.[28]

A few years later, Wallace was to develop his ideas on the extinction of inferior races in a chapter of his *Natural Selection* (1870), in which he even predicted the conclusion of the process in a distant but foreseeable future, when "the world is again inhabited by a single, nearly homogeneous race."[29]

The British anthropologist Benjamin Kidd declared in *Social Evolution,* one of the most widely diffused late-nineteenth-century summaries of social Darwinism, that it was utterly pointless for the white man to demonstrate his philanthropic virtues and his Christian ethics, since it was despite himself, thanks to an anthropological and historical law as inevitable as it was pitiless, that he was causing the end of the "savage peoples": "Whenever a superior race comes into close contact and competition with an inferior race, the result seems to be much the same," whether reached "by the rude methods of wars and conquest [or] the subtle, though no less efficient, methods with which science makes us acquainted."[30] So no purpose was served by attempts to elucidate the causes of "the extinction" (machine guns or diseases). Needless to say, the discourse of the British naturalists was matched by their colleagues in France, where social Darwinism exerted considerable influence on the development of anthropology. In 1888, Edmond Perrier wrote:

Human races owe their spread on earth to their superiority. Just as animals disappear before the advance of man, this privileged being, so too the savage is wiped out before the European, before civilization ever takes hold of him. However regrettable this may be from a moral point of view, civilization seems to have spread throughout the world far more by dint of destroying the barbarians than by subjecting them to its laws.[31]

It was Tasmania, the smallest of the Australian islands, that, toward the end of the nineteenth century, focused the fantasies of the imperialist culture. Edifying proof of this is provided by a book called *The Last of the Tasmanians,* in which James Bonwick, a sort of Bartolomeo de Las Casas of the Victorian age, recorded the various versions of the apology for genocide purveyed by the colonial press and literature of the time.[32] The demographic decline of populations brought about by the arrival of the colonists, with all their unknown viruses and infections (smallpox, measles, malaria, venereal diseases) the effect of which was to propagate epidemics and cause sterility, was inevitably interpreted by Western observers as confirmation of selectionist theories. An abundant literature in the main European languages set about introducing scientific categories for codifying the law of "the fatal impact" of civilization upon "savages." It was without doubt a "demographic law" that M. Marestang was attempting to prove in the *Revue scientifique* in 1892: "All inferior peoples put in contact with a superior people are fatally condemned to perish."[33] In 1909, E. Caillot was writing along the same lines in a work entitled *Les Polynésiens orientaux au contact de la civilisation*:

> When a people has remained stationary for so long, all hope of seeing it advance must be abandoned. It is bound to be classified among the inferior nations and, like these, is condemned to die out or be absorbed by a superior race. . . . That is the implacable law of nature against which nothing can prevail, as has repeatedly been established by history: the stronger devours the weaker. The Polynesian race did not manage to scale the rungs of the ladder of progress, it has added not the slightest contribution to the efforts that humanity has made to im-

prove its lot. It must therefore make way before others that are more worthy, and disappear. Its death will be no loss to civilization.[34]

The writings of Darwin are not altogether free of Eurocentric features of this kind, and there can be no doubt that, right from the first, *Origins of Species* (1859) was regarded as the decisive scientific justification for imperialistic practices.[35] It is now generally accepted that Darwin cannot be considered responsible for social Darwinism because of the affiliation that its representatives claim, using terms that are in many cases exaggerated or even distorting. However, to postulate a total separation between the two would be equally false. Despite its rejection of polygenicist theories of the origin of the species, the Darwinian view of the extra-European world was, as André Pichot puts it, a singular, basically very Victorian mixture of "the morality of the catechism" and "an utterly soulless colonialist racism."[36]

Darwin always shared his own age's dominant view of "inferior races," which were regarded as "living fossils," vestiges of a past destined to disappear as civilization progressed. In his "Notebook E" we find a passage dated December 1838 that would not have been out of place in *Mein Kampf*: "When two races of men meet, they act precisely like two species of animals—they fight, eat each other, bring diseases to each other, but then comes the most deadly struggle, namely which have the best fitted organization, or instincts (ie. intellect, in man) to gain the day."[37] The following year, he noted in his diary "a mysterious factor: wherever the European settles, death seems to persecute the aborigine."[38] This is a reference to a Western stereotype that Darwin did not invent but that he did not manage to avoid and that recurs constantly in those of his works that preceded the elaboration of his theory of natural selection. The theory, however, then enabled him to convert that "mysterious factor" to which he had alluded in 1839 into a veritable scientific law. In *The Descent of Man* (1871), he described the death of the natives of the British colonies as the inevitable consequence of the impact of civilization, which he took to be confirmation of his theory of natural selection. In short, he had no hesitation in applying the latter to a social phenomenon, thereby introducing a biologization of history and sanctioning the popularization of social Darwinism. Darwin meditated upon "the struggle between civilized nations and barbarian peoples," comparing the extinction of the "savage races" to that of the fossil horse, which the Spanish horse replaced in South America. His argument continues as follows: "The New Zealander seems conscious of this parallelism, for he compares his future fate with that of the native rat, now almost exterminated by the European rat." [39] In a note in which he quotes the naturalist Poepping, he describes "the breath of civilization as poisonous to savages." [40] A few years after the publication of *The Descent of Man,* the Austrian social Darwinist Ludwig Gumplowicz, for whom politics was simply an "applied science," abandoned the metaphors of his master and explained more precisely how it was that civilization revealed itself to be "poison" to "savages." He reminded the reader that the Boers considered "the men of the jungle and the Hottentots" to be "creatures" (*Geschöpfe*) that it was permissible to exterminate as game (*die man wie das Wild des Waldes ausrotten darf*).[41]

At the turn of the century, social Darwinism, eugenics, and theories of natural selection were to flourish particularly vigorously in America, where they were used to justify the genocide of the Indians and the rise of the United States as a major power on the international stage. In 1893 the historian Frederick Jackson Turner delivered his famous lecture on the significance of the frontier in American history. In it, he used the frontier, the source of two essential principles of the American nation, democracy and individualism, as a metaphor for progress, "the meeting point between savagery and civilization." [42] It represented the *limes* or boundary of progress, and as it pushed forward it wiped out backward indigenous populations: "The wild man must cease to exist," Turner declared. [43] The eugenicist J. K. Hosmer interpreted the accession of the United States to the rank of a major power as confirmation of the civilizing mission of the Anglo-Saxon culture: "English institutions, the English language, and English thought should become the principle features of the political, social, and intellectual life of the human race." [44] His colleague Josiah Strong announced a new era, that of "a final competition between the races," the natural consequence of which would be American hegemony. [45] One of the most enthusiastic and convinced partisans of social Darwinism and white supremacy was the president of the United States, Theodore Roosevelt, who in *The Winning of the West* wrote that he considered the Anglo-Saxons to be a branch of the Nordic race and interpreted the conquest of the American West as a prolongation of the expansion of the Germanic tribes, celebrating it as "the crowning achievement of this powerful history of racial development." [46] In the wake of Francis Galton and his work *Hereditary Genius,* Madison Grant proceeded to move beyond social Darwinism and adopt a biological determinism in which "natural selection" was to be replaced by an "artificial selection" of races. According to Grant, the destruction of the Indians had pointed the way, by showing that an effective policy for the elimination of the weak, those unsuited to civilization, and "degenerates" would eventually make it possible to "clear out the undesirables who fill our prisons, hospitals, and psychiatric asylums." [47]

But in nineteenth-century Western imaginary representations, it was Africa that became the favorite screen for the projection of colonial fantasies. Africa was a continent conquered but still strange and mysterious, totally exotic, the exploration of which was felt to be and was represented as a descent into

"the darkness of the earliest times." As such it attracted the attention of writers, scholars, missionaries, adventurers . . . It
provided an ideal mirror for the world that the West had "invented": a continent that, unlike India—which polarized the
attention of a European culture obsessed by the Aryan myth—
was quite naturally perceived as the refuge of primitive and
savage humanity. The place attributed to the Africans in the
racial typology established by Paul Broca, the founder of the
Société Anthropologique de Paris, is by now well known.[48] But
it will perhaps be helpful to record the view expressed in the
works of the British anthropologist William Winwood Reade,
an explorer and great traveler now remembered for his lengthy
correspondence with Darwin, for whom he provided extensive
material for *The Descent of Man.* In 1863, Reade published *Savage Africa,* a long account of his travels brimming with geographical and ethnological data, descriptions of tropical forests
and vast lakes, and also careful observations on local mores,
rounded off by a chapter devoted to the "redemption" of this
continent. After declaring that, faced with populations lacking
both written language and any kind of culture, slavery was "a
necessity,"[49] Reade predicted the future that awaited the continent, following a long period of French and British colonization.[50] Under the rule of these colonial powers, the Africans
would transform their continent into a kind of garden, building towns in the depths of the forests and irrigating the deserts.
After completing their task of inoculating this *"elixir vitae* into
the veins of their mother" and restoring her "immortal beauty,"
the Africans would be able to depart from the historical stage.
Reade's conclusion ran as follows: "In this amiable task they
may possibly become exterminated. We must learn to look on
this result with composure. It illustrates the beneficent law of
nature, that the weak must be devoured by the strong."[51] Reade
described this extermination in typically British understated
and sober terms, which in his final pages even took on bucolic

and nostalgic overtones. His book ends with a touching portrait that is worth recording: young girls seated on the banks of the Niger, described as a river as romantic as the Rhine, tearfully read a story entitled "The Last of the Negroes."

This huge debate on "the extinction of inferior races," which were described sometimes as "declining," sometimes as "dying," and were inevitably condemned to make way for Western civilization, continued throughout the second half of the nineteenth century. Analyzed retrospectively, it emerges as an extraordinarily rich arsenal of racial stereotypes—formulated in the language of science, morality, and the philosophy of history—that was part of the culture of imperialist and colonialist Europe. Far more than that, though, it illustrates the attempts to rationalize and provide ideological legitimation for a vast project of conquest and genocide.[52] Far from being the terrain of scholarly debates, concepts such as these deeply pervaded the political language of the period. In 1898, the British prime minister, Lord Salisbury, divided the world into two categories, "living nations and dying nations,"[53] and two years later Kaiser Wilhelm II delivered a passionate speech in which he urged the German soldiers sent to China to repress the Boxer revolt to exterminate the Boxers with all the violence shown by the Huns led by Attila.[54] Such discourse, unimaginable in relation to a European nation, reflected the practices commonly pursued by all the colonial powers.

## COLONIAL WARS AND CRIMES

Of course, colonial wars—"small wars," in the military jargon of the day—involved human and material resources on an incomparably smaller scale than those of World War II. They did not fundamentally undermine the social structures and relations of the European countries involved and the total number of their victims—at least those resulting directly from armed conflicts—was far lower than the millions who died in the 1914–1918 carnage. Nevertheless, the very concept of those earlier conflicts already rested upon the principle of total war. These were not the type of conflicts envisaged by international law, ones involving states hostile to each other but eventually resolved by peace treaties. Instead, they were undeclared wars of pillage and destruction that were brought to a conclusion only by the total submission of the conquered countries. The enemies were neither governments nor proper armies, but the populations themselves, which meant that no distinction was drawn between civilians and combatants.[55] That is why France's General Bugeaud used to tell his officers that in waging war in Algeria, they needed first to forget most of what they had learned in their French military academies and realize that their battle was "not against an enemy army, but against an enemy people."[56] It was in Africa that the European states for the first time made massive use of the machine guns and other automatic weapons that had been tested in the American Civil War. This military superiority was decisive in the colonization of Africa and, as a result of a few crucial battles, allowed the British South Africa Company to keep Rhodesia, General Lugard to remain in Uganda, and the Germans to retain Tanganyika. Military history textbooks referred frequently to the Battle of Omdurman in which, in 1898, a British unit numbering no more than a few hundred soldiers, under the command of Lord Kitchener and armed with modern machine guns, prevailed over thousands of Sudanese warriors, killing 11,000 of them[57] ("We shall mow them down like ripened wheat," the young Winston Churchill declared on the eve of the battle).[58] But over and above the superiority of the European armies—which only became overwhelming in the second half of the nineteenth century, when the far-reaching impact of the Industrial Revolution resulted in a qualitative transformation of military techniques—the secret of the colonial conquests lay in the rational organization of colonial military units, which were supported by an efficient administrative infrastructure, were kept constantly supplied, were regularly beefed up with fresh troops, and were able to maintain permanent links with the metropolis.[59]

In the long term, the catastrophic consequences of colonialism were to be revealed not on the battlefields, where all in all losses were limited, but throughout the conquered territories, as a result of a demographic decline that in a number of cases can only be described as genocide. The population of the present Sri Lanka before colonization was between 4 million and 10 million souls; by 1920, it had been reduced to about 1 million. Between 1830 and 1870, the Algerian population fell by 15 to 20 percent from about 3 million to 2.3 million. (Victor Hugo evoked this colonial war in highly imagistic terms: "Zaatcha, Tlamcen, Mascara: the army in Africa has become a tiger,"[60] while General Lapasset summed it up more simply but no less eloquently as "theft and spoliation."[61]) In the Congo, where the savage exploitation of King Leopold II's copper mines truly resembled a form of extermination through work,[62] the population was reduced by half between 1880 and 1920, from 20 million to 10 million. On the Ivory Coast the population went, between 1900 and 1910 from 1.5 million to 160,000. In Sudan, there was a 75-percent drop: in 1882, the first year of British colonization, there were between 8 million and 9 million inhabitants; by 1903 the population had been reduced to between 2 million and 3 million. In Tahiti and New Caledonia there was a 90-percent decline.[63] According to the most trustworthy calculations, the victims of the European conquests in Asia and Africa in the course of the second half of the nineteenth century numbered 50 million to 60 million, roughly half being due to the famine in India.[64]

The colonial wars waged by the Germans in South-West Africa at the beginning of the twentieth century had the fea-

tures of a campaign of extermination that prefigured Hitler's
1941 campaign in the USSR (albeit on a much smaller scale).[65]
In 1904 the repression of a revolt by the Hereros in what is now
Namibia assumed the aspect of a veritable genocide. General
von Trotha, the chief officer in command of the operation,
proudly claimed responsibility for issuing an "annihilation
order" (*Vernichtungsbefehl*) that became famous.[66] The German
authorities decided to take no prisoners among the combatants
and to do nothing for the remaining women and children.
These were simply moved away and abandoned in the desert.
The Herero population, which in 1904 had numbered about
80,000 people, had been reduced to fewer than 20,000 one year
later. Similar methods were employed to put down the Hotten-
tot revolt and resulted in halving the population, from 20,000 to
10,000.[67] In the course of the following years, General von
Trotha was to declare in several articles that the extermination
of the Hereros had been a "racial war" (*Rassenkampf*) waged
against peoples "in decline" (*untergehende Völker*) or even
"dying" (*sterbende*). He explained that in this struggle, the Darwinian law of "the survival of the fittest" proved to be a more
pertinent guide than international law.[68] In the debates that
took place in the Reichstag (German parliament) at the time,
the Nationalists loudly voiced their approval of the annihilation of the "savages" and "beasts" revolting in Africa against
colonial rule, while the Socialists, though anxious to avoid
mixed marriages in the colonies, stigmatized such episodes of
violence, which reduced the German imperial army to "a level
of bestiality worthy of its victims." Those debates prove that
notions such as "racial warfare," "extermination," and "subhu-
manity" were widespread in Germany under Kaiser Wilhelm
as a result of colonial policies.[69] Later, Nazism deliberately kept
the memory of this past alive by means of its editorial strategies
and the cinema. In 1941, just before unleashing war upon the
USSR, German cinemas were showing two colonial films re-

leased for the general public, *Carl Peters* and *Ohm Krüger*. On the opening night in the Berlin UFA-Palast, their importance was emphasized by the presence of Joseph Goebbels, the minister of propaganda.[70]

The last operation of colonial conquest, the Ethiopian war waged by the Italian Fascists in 1935, bridged the gap between nineteenth-century European imperialism and the Nazi war for German Lebensraum. The Ethiopian war was justified by the classic arguments of colonialist racism ("Africa can never belong to the Africans") and by demographic discourse of the social Darwinist variety ("only fertile peoples with the pride and the will to propagate their race upon this planet have the right to an empire") and was waged with modern tools of destruction, in particular a massive use of chemical weapons.[71] In June 1936, Mussolini ordered Rodolfo Graziani, the commander of military operations in Ethiopia, to "pursue a systematic policy of terror and extermination against the rebels and all accomplice populations."[72] Between 1935 and 1939, Ethiopian resistance was broken by warfare that combined conventional and chemical weapons and caused the death of 250,000 "natives." The Fascists' long-term aim was to direct Italian emigration toward the African colonies. Alessandro Lessona, the minister for colonies, dreamed of an "Ethiopia without Ethiopians," populated by Italians and organized in conditions of apartheid, on the basis of a veritable segregation of the indigenous population.[73] The anti-Semitic dimension of the racial laws promulgated by the regime in 1938 may have been the most visible and the most laden with consequences within Italian society, but those laws stemmed from the Fascist insistence on "separating" Italians from the "natives" in African colonies.[74] A number of historians have used the term "genocide" to describe this Fascist colonial war.[75] The photographs that show Italian soldiers brandishing the severed heads of Ethiopian resistance fighters may certainly be compared, in terms of cruelty, to those, better known today, that testify to the activities of the Wehrmacht in Poland and the Soviet Union.

## NAZISM AND "LEBENSRAUM"

The Nazi war against the USSR illustrates the historical links between the Hitlerian *weltanschauung* and the European colonialism of the nineteenth century. The German blitzkrieg of 1941 condensed all the aims of the Nazis, among which the desire to eliminate the USSR and Communism was indissociable from the acquisition of *Lebensraum,* a "living space" for Germany in eastern Europe. The Nazi General Plan Ost (General Plan for the East), developed cooperatively by several research centers using the services of numerous geographers, economists, demographers, and specialists in the "racial sciences,"[76] envisaged the German colonization of the territories extending all the way from Leningrad to the Crimea. A few alterations were made to this plan after the beginning of the blitzkrieg against the USSR and before the collapse of the Wehrmacht in 1943, but its major objectives remained clearly defined. The first stage involved evacuating—through the deportment or elimination of about 30 million to 40 million "racially undesirable" (*rassisch unerwünscht*) Slavs; over the next thirty or so years, about 10 million Germans and ethnic Germans (*Volksdeutsche, Deutschstämmige*) were gradually to be installed, to colonize the conquered territories and rule over the Slavs, who would be reduced to slavery (*Heloten*). The extermination of "races" judged to be harmful, such as the Jews and the Gypsies, was part of the overall plan and was to be completed during the conflict.[77] In November 1941, during the German offensive against the USSR, Göring, in the course of conversations with the Italian minister of foreign affairs, Galeazzo Ciano, said that he foresaw that 20 million to 30 million Soviet citizens would be affected by famine in the course of the following year.[78] The

Wehrmacht's advance implied the systematic pillaging of all occupied territories. The Jews, who were considered to hold the power in the USSR and to be the brains behind the international Communist movement, were an essential target of the Nazi war. The key to the extreme violence and brutality of this war certainly lies in this (political and racial) synthesis of conquest and extermination.[79]

At the legal level, expansionism in the East and the war of conquest were justified by Carl Schmitt in an essay written in 1941 and devoted to the concept of *Grossraum,* to which we shall return later in this book. Schmitt recognized that the war then being waged called into question principles of international law, but he added that it was part of the expansionist tendency followed outside Europe by the great powers, upon which it was based. European law, the broad lines of which had been laid down from the sixteenth century onward, was designed to establish a European geopolitical order based upon an underlying postulate: colonial expansion outside Europe. Schmitt wrote:

> The non-European space was without masters [*herrenlos*], uncivilized or only semi-civilized, a territory for colonization and the object of conquest by European powers which thereby became empires, thanks to their colonies overseas. So far, the colonies have been the spatial element upon which European law is founded.[80]

Portugal, Spain, Great Britain, France, and the Netherlands had all managed to build their empires. Prussia had not, so its territorial expansion could only be achieved "at the expense of the neighbors, who belonged, legally, to the European community."[81]

In substance, said Schmitt, German imperialism upset the European balance and attacked its laws, but its action was certainly in line with the Western tendency. In other words, the

Germans were simply applying in Poland, Ukraine, the Baltic States, and Russia exactly the same principles and methods as those already adopted by France and the United Kingdom in Africa and Asia.

In conversations with Martin Bormann in 1941–42, Hitler frequently compared the German war on the eastern front to the colonial wars. The Slavic world had to be conquered and colonized so as to turn it into a sort of "Germanic India," and its population had to be put down using methods of destruction comparable to those employed by the English in their empire and the Americans against the Indian tribes. The enslavement of the Slavic peoples and the extermination of the Gypsies and, above all, the Jews were regarded to be aspects of a process for which the European conquests in Africa and Asia and the Indian wars in America's Far West provided the model. They were in line with a historical trend in which Nazi policies, which expressed a somewhat delayed imperialism, found their justification and natural place. Hitler, like other Nazi ideologues such as Alfred Rosenberg, made no secret of his admiration of Great Britain and even of Churchill (before Churchill became "corrupted" by Anglo-American Judaism), and praised the latter's "pride," which stemmed from a sense of racial superiority and an awareness of the "imperial mission" of Great Britain.[82] Thanks to the writings of Houston Stewart Chamberlain (1855–1927), a Wagnerian racist of English origin, he had learned to draw a distinction between the old, aristocratic, colonial Great Britain of Burke and Gladstone and the modern, merchant, materialist kingdom, which was the very embodiment of *Zivilisation* and was spiritually opposed to Germany.[83] In the early stages of the war Hitler continued to hope to reach an agreement with the British, on the basis of an "equitable" deal: German respect for British maritime hegemony in return for acceptance of German domination in continental Europe.

In August 1941, at the beginning of the offensive against the USSR, Hitler said, "What India was for England, the eastern territories will be for us."[84] In September he again declared, "If the English were to be ejected, India would waste away. Our role in the East will be analogous to that of the English in India."[85] It was a comparison that resurfaced constantly in his conversations during those crucial years, in which British imperialism was set up as a model: "It must be possible to dominate that Eastern region with 250,000 men led by good administrators. Let us follow the example of the English, who, with 250,000 men in all, of whom 50,000 are soldiers, rule over 400 million Indians. The Eastern space must be ruled in perpetuity by the Germans."[86] Around mid-October 1941, as the German armies reached the gates of Leningrad, Hitler was indulging in dreams of an Eastern Europe vanquished by Germany, dreams that inevitably call to mind the African fantasies of Winwood Reade: "In twenty years' time Ukraine will already have twenty million inhabitants apart from its native peoples. In three hundred years that country will be one of the finest gardens in the world."[87] Completion of this "civilizing mission" inevitably entailed the extinction of "natives," as a result of a process similar to the conquest of the American Far West. "The natives will have to be shot. . . . Our sole duty is to Germanize the country by the immigration of Germans, regarding the natives as Redskins."[88] In 1942 he compared the German repression of resistance in the occupied territories to "the war waged on the Indians in North America."[89] The "natives" were not to be Germanized but simply reduced to slavery. By extending his comparison of the Slavs of the Lebensraum to the Indians in the English colonies and the populations of Mexico before their conquest by Cortes, Hitler transformed them into non-Europeans. He excluded the idea of "educating" them, for that could only be "to the detriment of the whites."[90] Conflating the Slavs with the "savages" of colonial imagery also cropped up in other conversations about the methods to be adopted for the colonization of the East. Hitler suggested teaching them a "language of gestures," banning literature, and prohibiting instruction; the radio would suffice to provide the masses with amusement, "as much music as they want."[91] The colonization of the Slavic world obviously implied the elimination of the political, military, administrative, and intellectual elites of a number of occupied countries.

The colonial nature of the war was impressed upon the German soldiers. In his work on "the European Civil War," Ernst Nolte cites the testimony of Erich Koch, the redoubtable Reich commissioner for the Ukraine, who declared that he had waged a colonial war "as among Negroes."[92] The German military hammered home the final aims that the Nazi world attributed to the war against the USSR. Omer Bartov, one of the principal historians of the Wehrmacht, has analyzed the indoctrination of this army. Its central elements, after the annihilation of the Jews and the eradication of Bolshevism, were the struggle to win *Lebensraum* and the defense of the West. Shortly before Operation Barbarossa (the code name for the invasion of the USSR), General Hoepner had written that "the war against Russia is an essential element in the German people's struggle for existence. It is the age-old struggle of the German tribes against the Slavs, the defense of European culture against the Moscovite-Asiatic invasion, resistance to Jewish Bolshevism."[93] The propaganda aimed at the Wehrmacht soldiers on the eastern front painted a terrifying picture of the political commissars of the Red Army, representing them in one pamphlet as "the flayers of human beings." This Nazi pamphlet went on to declare that "the figure cut by these commissars testifies to a revolt of *Untermenschen* against noble blood."[94] In the last year of the war, the regime gave up trying to weld the army together around the prospect of victory, as it had in 1941, and attempted to do so by appealing to the defense of the West under threat. A directive to Nazi Wehrmacht officers summarized the goals of the war as follows: "1. Asia has never conquered Europe. We shall once again break the advance of this Asiatic tide. 2. The domination of Asiatic subhumans over the West is unnatural and contradicts the sense of history. 3. Behind the wave of the Red masses, the rictus of the Jew is detectable. His thirst for domination will be broken, as his power in Germany has been."[95] A last echo of this propaganda still lingers in contemporary historiography, for example in the works of Andreas Hillgruber, who has presented the struggle of the Wehrmacht (in which he served) in the last year of the war as a desperate and tragic attempt to defend the populations of eastern Germany against the onslaught of Slavic barbarity, "against vengeance, collective rape, arbitrary assassination, and the countless deportations" perpetrated by the Red Army.[96] At the time of the *Historikerstreit,* Jürgen Habermas was an unyielding critic of this apologetic orientation, which on the basis of a selective sympathy with the eastern Germans (but not the victims of Nazism) led Hillgruber to continue to support the arguments of Nazi propaganda.[97]

Deportation, dehumanization, and racial extermination as undertaken by Hitler's Germany are in line with earlier ideas that were firmly anchored in the history of Western imperialism. The fact that National Socialism was the first to envisage a policy of extermination within Europe itself, targeting nations of the Old World, and in particular a people active at the origins of Western civilization, does not negate the connection. The "logical and factual precedent" for Nazi crimes is to be found in colonial wars, not in Bolshevik Russia.[98] The connection, all too frequently obscured, nevertheless must be qualified. Nazi expansionism crossed a new threshold when it altered the hierarchy of the codes of classic imperialism. The imperialists occupied territories in order to pillage them, to seize their raw

THE ORIGINS OF NAZI VIOLENCE · 74

materials, conquer new markets, and "extend civilization," and
to that end they needed to postulate the rationale of the Europeans' superiority over those colonized and if necessary to subject the latter to a policy of extermination. Nazism subscribed
to the same logic, but the central and primary goal of its expansionism was to extend German domination on the basis of biological and racist claims. It was a matter not just of conquering
territories, but of Germanizing them. For Nazism, eugenics
and racism constituted far more than a justification and ideological cover for an expansionist policy: they were its very
motor.[99] Consequently we must define the historical analogy
more precisely; if it is reduced to a mechanical transposition of
nineteenth-century imperialism to Nazi expansionism, there is
a danger that a number of essential and specific aspects of the
Hitlerian vision of the world (to which we shall be returning
below) will be lost. The Nazi regime envisaged a colonial solution to the "Jewish question" in 1940, at the moment of the defeat of France: a massive deportation of Jews to Madagascar
that would coincide with the installation of *Volksdeutsch* groups
in the occupied territories of eastern Europe. The plan was
abandoned one year later, when the project of extermination
became part of the offensive against the USSR.

In contrast to the imperialist view of the colonized, Nazism
did not regard the Jews as a backward, savage, primitive people
or one that was incapable of surviving the onward march of
progress. It considered them not as an archaic element that had
lingered on the path of civilization but as civilization's *enemy*.
In a famous speech, "Communism Unmasked" ("Kommunis-
mus ohne Maske"), delivered in September 1935, shortly before
the passage of the Nuremberg Laws, Joseph Goebbels described the Jews as the guides of an "internationale of subhumans" hostile to culture (*Kultur*).[100] In July 1941, at the
beginning of the war against the USSR, the minister of propaganda produced an article reiterating his view of the German

mission. For him, the soldiers of the Reich were the "saviors" (*Erretter*) of European civilization, which was under threat from a "political underworld" directed by the Jews.[101] In 1942, the SS distributed 4 million copies of a pamphlet entitled *Der Untermensch,* in which the Jews were represented as the brains behind a state of subhumans.[102] Their elimination was no longer of an instrumental nature (conquest), but took on the grandiose dimension of a struggle for *regeneration* that Goebbels liked to describe as "an action of historic world importance ([*eine*] *welthistorische Tat*)."[103] The Nazi destruction of the Jews cannot be reduced simply to a measure of racial or social prophylaxy, let alone to a process of "natural extinction," for it was conceived and organized as a crusade, a war of liberation.[104] Eastern Europe certainly represented a "living space," to be colonized, but that conquest implied the annihilation of the USSR and Bolshevism, a state and an ideology that the Nazis considered to be the product of an alliance between the "Jewish intelligentsia" and the Slavic "subhumans."[105] The Red Army was the embodiment of this threatening alliance. Crushing it required measures quite different from those deployed in the nineteenth-century colonial expeditions: what was needed now was nothing less than "total war" in the heart of Europe. The Jewish genocide was conceived and realized as part of that total war, a war of conquest that was both "racial" and colonial, and extremely radical.

# 3

# *Destruction:*
# *Total War*

## THE FORDIST ARMY

The first truly "total war" of the democratic age and the society of the masses was the Great War, in which 13 million men perished. It was the founding act of the twentieth century. In August 1914, it was acclaimed in most European capitals as an opportunity to affirm the values of the nationalist ethos (virility, strength, courage, heroism, and *union sacrée*) in the purificatory fire of warfare. But its violence was to submerge the whole world. The intoxication of patriotism gave way before the discovery of the modern horrors of anonymous mass slaughter, industrialized massacre, bombed towns, and ravaged countrysides. The "fields of honor" acquired a new face: trenches stretching for hundreds of miles in which soldiers crouched for months on end in the mud, surrounded by barbed wire and, often, corpses and rats.

A far cry from the mythical image of the hero, soldiers now became a proletariat, workers in the service of a war machine. Stripped of the aura of the ancient warrior, soldiers were subjected to a military discipline in every way comparable to that of industrial production. The "worker masses" of a Ford-type factory were now matched by the "soldier masses" of modern armies.[1] Hierarchy, obedience to orders, and the segmentation of tasks made it impossible for soldiers to understand, let alone control, the overall strategy within the context of which they operated. They waged war like workers on a production line, in a context in which fighting had lost all epic dimensions and been converted into a planned mass slaughter. The army as a whole was converted into a rationalized, mechanical business, with a hierarchy and a bureaucracy, and separate, coordinated sectors in which tasks were distributed on a strictly functional basis. As we have noted above, Marx had compared the industrial workers of the nineteenth century to soldiers. In World War I that model was reversed: now the army adopted the principles of a rationalized factory. The soldiers who manned machine guns were not elite marksmen but automata who, like factory workers on a production line, simply fed their weapons with ammunition. The military historian John Keegan has observed that "the machine-gun . . . *mechanized* or *industrialized* the act of killing."[2] Veterans have described the war as "an endless industrial process."[3]

The Great War marked an essential point in the diffusion of Taylorism in Europe.[4] Economy ministers adopted Taylorism in both Germany (Walther Rathenau) and France (Albert Thomas). The mobilization of young men at the Front made it necessary to recruit a new workforce that was unskilled—women and adolescents—to work in the munitions factories, and so was perfectly adapted to the Taylorist model of "scientific management." In the army, the ergonomists, hygienists, and psychologists of work found a productive field in which to try out their hypotheses on the disciplining of bodies, the organization of space, and psychotechniques. Specialists of the disorders linked with fatigue resulting from industrial labor—neuroses, cataplexy, and so on—made close studies of soldiers exhausted by life in the trenches or suffering from shell shock, who provided them with a vast field in which to test their theories.[5] Medical vocabulary was enriched by new expressions such as "shell shock" and "war hysteria" that entered into common speech.[6] Engineers and psychotechnicians prepared for the reabsorption of mutilated men into industrial production. Just as chronometers now ruled the rationalized factories, in the army modern relations between bodies and machines and time and space called for strict coordination and calculations. On the morning of July 1, 1916, at 7:30 A.M., the start of the Battle of the Somme was signaled by whistle blasts from hundreds of unit commanders who had all synchronized their watches.[7]

In 1918, Max Weber highlighted the features that state administrations, factories, and armies all had in common in modern societies. The officer caste had been bureaucratized; it was now simply "a particular category of officials [*Beamten*], nothing like the knights and 'condottieri' of the past or the Homeric leaders and heroes."[8] In all the three domains Weber pointed to the same "separation of the worker from the material means of operations: from the means of production in the economy, from the tools of warfare (*Kriegsmittel*) in the army, and from the material means of management in public administration."[9] Just as, in business, leadership, programming, and production had become separate, hierarchized operations, in the army, strategy was now the task of a stratum of generals and officers always physically absent from the front line. In polar contrast to the warriors of earlier times, officers now hardly bore arms at all. "Officers do not kill" for "killing is not the business of a gentleman": that was one of the principles most solidly rooted in the system of military values in the period of total warfare.[10]

Technological warfare was the outcome of a tendency that had been gathering force ever since the nineteenth century's Industrial Revolution. Between the introduction of conical bullets in 1840 and of the modern machine gun in 1918, firearms had evolved considerably. Around the mid-nineteenth century, bronze had begun to be replaced by steel in the fabrication of cannons that no longer used the old, solid cannon balls but instead used explosive shells, which were much quicker to load. By 1861, the American multibarreled Gatling gun, soon copied in several European countries, ensured rapid, continuous, and prolonged fire. This weapon automatically completed in a single cycle all the operations previously executed separately— releasing the firing pin, opening the bolt, ejecting the cartridge, loading the new round, and locking it into place, making it possible to fire between 550 and 700 rounds a minute. By the end of the century it had become much smaller and easier to handle and move. But it was not until the outbreak of war, in 1914, that military leaders came to realize what changes this technical revolution implied on the battlefield. The extraordinary power of these new firearms had not yet been taken into consideration strategically. Staff headquarters were still assigning a crucial role to the cavalry and the infantry. In 1907, British military handbooks were confidently declaring that even the most modern rifles would never bear comparison with the speed and "magnetism" of a cavalry charge.[11] In 1914, a soldier's equipment differed hardly at all from that of the first half of the nineteenth century: officers' uniforms testified to preoccupations with aesthetics rather than function, and soldiers did not yet wear helmets (not until the following year were these introduced by all armies). The firepower of machine guns had certainly been tested in Africa at the time of the colonial wars, but the racist prejudices of the military leaders had prevented them from drawing full conclusions from the experience. To them machine guns seemed useful when pointed at Hereros or Zulus but not suitable as replacements for traditional weaponry in a European war. The staff headquarters, solid bastions of the aristocratic strata and the very embodiment of the "enduring Ancien Régime," thus persisted in launching bayonet charges involving hundreds of thousands of soldiers who were regularly scythed down by the fire of automatic weapons. There was no chance of anybody's heeding one Matabele warrior's account of his first encounter with a British unit's machine guns, that they "fired bullets as the sky emits flashes of lightning."[12] Yet his testimony proved a fair enough description of the experience of hundreds of thousands of soldiers in Europe during World War I.[13] The mass mutinies provoked by the massacres that occurred when bayonet charges were launched were repressed by martial law and a wave of executions, many of them by machine-gun decimation—methods similar to those used in the colonial wars against African tribes. The shocking discrepancy between the strategic ideas of the military elite and the reality of total warfare was eventually rectified at the technical level by the introduction of tanks, and was reflected within the military hierarchy by the replacement of those in command of operations: Lloyd-George replaced Lord Asquith; Clemenceau replaced Viviani; Hindenburg and Ludendorff replaced Bethmann-Hollweg; and Diaz replaced Cadorna.[14]

## MASS ANONYMOUS DEATH

The face of battle was changing. The rapid, violent military clashes of the nineteenth century were replaced by trench warfare. Offensives could last for months, mobilized hundreds of thousands of soldiers, were supported by an imposing logistic apparatus, and invariably became operations for the planned destruction of the enemy (which also implied huge losses for the assailants). Warfare became an industrialized form of extermination, far exceeding the technical and moral limits within which it had been described by Carl von Clausewitz a century earlier in *On War*.[15] According to one German volunteer writing from the front, the most terrible aspect of this war was that everything had become mechanical: "You could almost describe it as an industry specializing in human butchery."[16] John Reed,

a newspaper correspondent who had already covered the
Balkan Wars and the Mexican Revolution, was assigned to the
Western Front from which he reported in 1915 that he was
watching "a war between industrial workshops" in which "the
trenches are factories that produce ruination, the ruination of
spirits as much as of bodies, veritable death."[17] During the last
years of the war, Ernst Jünger wrote in *Total Mobilization:*
"Countries were transformed into gigantic factories for the
mass production of armies in order that, twenty-four hours out
of twenty-four, it would be possible to send them to the Front,
where a bloody consumer-process, likewise completely mechanized, played the role of the market."[18] Refashioned by the material structures and cultural codes of industrial society, modern
warfare was conceived as a gigantic business the purpose of
which, paradoxically, was the planned annihilation of the
enemy and the success of which could be measured by the extent
of the massacre. Henri Barbusse had described the soldiers of
1914–18 as "destruction workers" (*ouvriers de la destruction*), and
similar formulations are to be found in the war recollections of
Ernst Jünger and Arnold Zweig (*Arbeiler der Zerstörung*).[19] In
such conditions death became "banal." It lost its epic character—
"death on the field of honor"—and took on the typically modern
aspect of anonymous mass slaughter.[20] The hero in this war was
not the soldier who, by virtue of his courage, qualities, and distinction, emerged from anonymity and entered the fellowship of
Olympian heroism; instead he was, the "unknown soldier." As
Roger Caillois pointed out, "Now public veneration went to the
poor wretch whose body had been the most disfigured and was
the most completely broken, the one whose smashed countenance, no longer recognizably human, could not possibly resemble any face from the past, nor evoke any individual in any
memory. That, indeed, was his sole virtue."[21] The Unknown
Soldier, whose anonymity was his sole claim to fame, was cho-
sen at random from among a number of mutilated corpses. His

selection was a matter of pure chance. This, Caillois insisted, was "the end of heroic warfare." [22]

The enemy, dehumanized, became invisible. He was close by but hidden in his trench. "This war is a war of invisibility," the art critic Camille Mauclair declared in 1918.[23] "Hand-to-hand fighting is a thing of the past," Jean Norton Cru stressed, having analyzed the testimony of veterans. With "an enemy who remained invisible," warfare became a terrible slaughter carried out amid a "total absence of hatred." [24] Very often death was dealt, not by an enemy of flesh and blood, but by an impersonal, cold, alien, hostile machine.[25] It was brought by mechanical monsters (tanks, planes, heavy artillery), by gas discharged by chemical weapons, or by flame throwers. Amid this apocalyptic landscape, the soldiers in their helmets and gas masks had the air of artificial, mechanical figures stripped of all humanity, as some of Otto Dix's engravings show. In the memoirs of war veterans, the anonymity of the enemy is frequently described as a chilling phenomenon. Warfare against these ungraspable enemies introduced an *anthropological break,* revealing a new perception of human life that essentially paved the way for the genocides of the future.[26] The Great War itself could certainly not be apprehended as genocide. But even as he recognizes this, John Keegan is forced to admit that there was "something about the massacres of the Somme that calls to mind Treblinka." On July 1, 1916, the British suffered 60,000 casualties in the space of a few hours, 21,000 of them fatal. By October 18 of the same year, when the offensive was officially over, the death toll among the Anglo-French forces was calculated to be as high as 600,000, and the Germans had suffered comparable losses.[27] The war turned armies into factories that produced death. The destruction of the enemy took place in accordance with the modalities of a system of production, as if conceived following the very same paradigm which, since 1913, had provided the basis for the manufacture of automobiles in

Henry Ford's American factories. The metaphor of the "worker" created by Ernst Jünger in 1932 in *The Worker* (*Der Arbeiter*) strikingly conveyed the fusion of the soldier and the factory worker realized by modern total warfare.[28] And that warfare introduced a principle that was to lead to its paroxysmic culmination in the gas chambers of the Nazi camps. From this point of view it is probably fair enough to represent Auschwitz as the most tragic of all illustrations of "the excesses of *homo faber.*"[29]

Total warfare engendered a new concept of glory that was a very far cry from the myth of death on the field of honor and that was to produce split human beings, inured to the schizophrenic coexistence of normality and murder. In some cases, the theaters, cafés, and restaurants of town centers were situated a mere few dozen miles behind the front line. Officers on leave, having breakfasted in their trenches, could that same evening be dining in a restaurant.[30] Men who in civilian life were respectable, peaceful citizens, worthy fathers and husbands, as soldiers at the front had to become killers, and this metamorphosis was glorified as the vocation and mission of every true patriot.[31] This plural, heterogeneous temporality that the war introduced into the European social space—the term "noncontemporaneous," as used by Ernst Bloch, seems appropriate—was to have long-term consequences.[32] It was in the trenches of the Great War that a new ethic and mentality were forged, without which the massacres of World War II would have been inconceivable. The first world conflict did not produce crimes comparable to those perpetrated in Poland between 1941 and 1943 by *Einsatzgruppen* supported by the "ordinary men" of German police battalions,[33] but the anomalous and perverse coexistence of normality and destruction, of civilized behavior and murder, certainly paved the way for such crimes.

## SOLDIERS, CIVILIANS, AND
## CONCENTRATION CAMPS

The "total" nature of the 1914–18 war, which lay at the origin of a transformation of modes of life and perceptions of time and the world for large swathes of society, did not stem solely from the vast scale of the human forces and materials that were mobilized. The dimension of "total warfare" also resulted from the fact that the boundary between the battlefield and civilian society was effaced. The theater of military operations extended over entire regions where the local populations became military targets.[34] Although on a far smaller scale than in World War II, the bombing of towns, the internment of nationals of enemy countries, and the deportation and forced labor of civilians marked a turning point in social relations and crossed a new threshold in the escalation of violence. Primitive practices assumed to have been banished forever, such as the taking of civilian hostages, reappeared and were compounded by the most modern inventions of chemical warfare. The principles of the state of law were suspended, and nationals of enemy countries were treated as prisoners of war. Sixty thousand Austro-Germans, Ottomans, and Bulgarians were interned in French territories; over 10,000 foreigners from Triple Entente powers—Great Britain, France, and Russia—were interned in Germany; 100,000 Belgian and French civilians were deported to Germany, and 100,000 Serbian civilians to the Austro-Hungarian Empire.[35] Unlike soldiers, interned and deported civilians were not protected by the law. As representatives of the Red Cross from neutral countries meeting at a congress in Geneva put it, they constituted "a novelty of this war; international treaties had not foreseen them."[36] Hannah Arendt described this mass of pariahs as "stateless people" who were not guilty of transgressing the law but nevertheless objectively found themselves outlawed and therefore without its protection. She detected in this phenomenon—which was to assume considerable proportions following the 1919 peace treaties—one of the essential conditions of modern genocides, the victims of which were human beings deprived of a legal existence and consequently deemed "superfluous." [37]

As for prisoners of war, they became forced laborers. The Great War witnessed a massive diffusion of the "concentrationary" phenomenon, which had first evolved in South Africa for the internment of Boer civilians at the beginning of the century during the Boer War. Between 1914 and 1918, the expression "concentration camps" entered the vocabulary of Western countries. To be sure, from the point of view of the South African camps' purpose, the criteria for the selection of detainees, the living conditions to which these people were subjected, and the resulting mortality rate, there is no common measure between them and the KZ of Nazi Germany or the camps of Stalin's Gulag. Nevertheless, with their wooden huts and their electrified barbed-wire fences, they presented a scene that would become all too familiar to millions of human beings over the next decades. During World War I, internment camps for displaced civilian populations and above all concentration camps for prisoners of war multiplied. By 1916 there were several hundred of them, scattered not only throughout Europe but also in India, Japan, Australia, Canada, and several African countries. Initially they had constituted a response to the need to provide somewhere to keep an ever-increasing number of prisoners (by January 1915, these already numbered 600,000 in Germany) within the framework of a war that was lasting much longer than had been foreseen, but soon they became fixed institutions, to which the military and political authorities tried to attribute a function at once disciplinarian and productive. With the introduction of the economic blockade against the Central Powers in 1915, the conditions of detention deteriorated so much for prisoners that the parcels of food and cloth-

ing sent by their families and the assistance organizations of
their native countries in many cases became essential for their
survival. In the poorest countries where support from families
that were mostly illiterate or semiliterate was limited, detention conditions were horrifying. Of the 600,000 Italian prisoners of war captured by the armies of the Central Powers
between 1915 and 1918, close to 100,000 perished in the camps
from cold, tuberculosis, and hunger.[38] The testimony of a Red
Cross nurse sent to work in the Ljubljana camp in 1917, following Caporetto's defeat, sounds strikingly like descriptions of
the "Moslems"—inmates suspended between life and death—
given by survivors from the Nazi camps: "There were about
300 of them, all in rags, filthy, and famished. They were like living skeletons moved by the force of inertia, in an unconscious
state, by now insensible to any manifestation of civilian life or
any memories."[39] In the Great War such experiences were exceptional and, above all, were not part of any planned strategy
of dehumanization and annihilation. But they did constitute a
field of experimentation for the concentration systems of the
Nazis and of Stalin. The camps were a synthesis of prison and
army, being at once places of disciplinary training (involving
corporal punishments, privation, subjugation) and of labor.
The prisoners were deployed in all kinds of productive activities such as tree felling and road or railway construction. Frequently the army hired them out as cheap labor, a procedure
that the Todt Organization generalized and perfected in
World War II. They were an unforeseen product of total warfare, made possible by the rationalization of armies and representing an important stage along the path that was to lead
Europe from the prisons of the nineteenth century to the concentration camps of totalitarian regimes.[40]

## WAR MEMORY

In the testimony provided by 1914–18 survivors, the image of death stands out as central to the experience of war. The trenches are described as cemeteries, the battle-scarred landscape is often evoked by an allegory, one of *hell,* which is strikingly similar to the descriptions of survivors of the Nazi concentration camps.[41] Other similarities, too, leap to the mind in the accounts of these survivors. First, the nauseous smell of death: the stench of the burned flesh in the extermination camps and of rotting corpses that assailed soldiers even before the front line came into sight. Then, the indescribable nature of the lived experience, the distance that separated it from the spoken or written word intended to reconstruct it. Primo Levi, along with many other deportees, was obsessed by that realization in the frequently recurring dreams of the Auschwitz nights, in which they tried to describe Auschwitz to their friends and families who, however, refused to listen: "They had returned home and with passion and relief were describing their past sufferings, addressing themselves to a loved person, and were not believed, indeed were not even listened to."[42] The reminiscences of survivors of the Great War are full of similar observations. For the German artist Franz Marc, the war was "a gigantic battle that words will never be able to describe."[43] For another painter, Paul Nash, the sight of the front was "absolutely indescribable." For H. H. Cooper, "The stench from the swollen corpses was beyond description." For Robert Graves, the periods of leave were indissociable from a deep unease: "The idea of being and staying at home was terrible, for one was surrounded by people who could not understand that reality."[44] The letters from Italian soldiers are studded with similar remarks, often written with spelling mistakes and clumsy turns of phrase but also with all the tang and authenticity of the language of the popular classes, impossible to render in translation: the war is "beyond imagination"; "everything is black and blood"; "I will not describe the battle as I am not allowed to and anyway you could not understand it, so you must simply imagine that there, where it took place, it was total destruction"; "I felt I was at the cinema."[45] One officer wrote: "The war has etched upon everyone a mark of suffering that effaces individual features, the only eloquent expression of it is the silence that dominates them all."[46] Paul Fussell believes that this gap between words and things was not caused by a failure of language, an absence of words to describe the reality. It was a matter not of language, but of rhetoric: the impossible task of making the war, this war, understandable to anyone who had not lived it.[47] In consequence, soldiers often cloaked themselves in silence, a silence that anticipated that of those who survived the extermination camps. In *The Drowned and the Saved,* Levi describes himself as a "bad" witness, precisely because he emerged alive from Auschwitz: "The history of the Lagers has been written almost exclusively by those who, like myself, never fathomed them to the bottom. Those who did so did not return, or their capacity for observation was paralyzed by suffering and incomprehension."[48] Similar sentiments were expressed by those who witnessed death in the trenches and in no-man's-land. The American poet Louis Simpson writes: "For an infantryman, war is a totally physical fact. That is why so many remain speechless when they think of the war. They feel that language falsifies physical life and betrays those who suffered its ultimate experience: death."[49] In his 1936 essay on the figure of the narrator in the work of Nicolas Leskov, Walter Benjamin represented the Great War as the crucial moment of a break in tradition in modern societies. As a consequence of that break, ancestral forms for the transmission of memories were abandoned; stories were suddenly relegated among the vestiges of a bygone age; it was now impossible for lived experience to be communicated in a form that could be perpetrated and enriched by being passed on by word of mouth. Benjamin wrote as follows: "The World War began an evolution that has been continuing ever since. At the time of the Armistice, did we not notice that people returned speechless from the battlefield, not richer in communicable experience, but poorer?" He then explained that the reason for this was that the war had radically undermined acquired experience, in particular "bodily experience, through material battle [*Materialschlacht*]": "A generation that had still been going to school travelling in a horse-drawn tram found itself out in the open without protection in a landscape where nothing was recognizable, except the clouds, and, there in the middle of a force-field invaded by destruction, tensions and explosions, stood the tiny, fragile human body."[50] Except in a few rare cases, painting was struck by that same "silence" and artists were paralyzed both during and after the Great War when faced with the task of representing the death that was indissociable from total warfare. That experience brought about "a break between contemporary history and painting."[51]

### LIVES UNWORTHY OF LIFE

In order to apprehend warfare of annihilation, German soldiers had coined the term *Verwüstungsschlag*, a word that Stéphane Andouin-Rouzeau and Annette Becker have aptly translated as "blasting," "destruction," "devastation."[52] Military strategists were also beginning to speak of "warfare of annihilation" (*Vernichtungskrieg*), a neologism that was to occupy a central place in Nazi vocabulary.[53] In retrospect, World War I can thus be seen as a laboratory of totalitarian violence, and, as Omar Bartov has pointed out, it was on its battlefields that the future architects of the Final Solution underwent their "baptism of fire."[54] The transformations of our mental world that that war engendered included an inurement to violent death and an indifference to human life that brought into question a number of past achievements—banishing torture, respect for the lives of prisoners and civilian populations—that had been considered irreversible since the Enlightenment.[55] National Socialists found a sadly famous formula, filtered by the language of eugenics, to codify new devaluation of human life: *lebensunwertes Leben,* "life unworthy to be lived." George L. Mosse cites a striking contrast to illustrate this turning point: In 1903, the town of Kishinev, in the Tsarist empire, was the scene of a terrible pogrom in which about three hundred Jews had been killed. This massacre aroused indignation and reprobation from worldwide public opinion, which was scandalized by such a barbaric episode. In contrast, the genocide of a million and a half Armenians under the Ottoman Empire during World War I provoked no significant level of protest.[56] Europe had become accustomed to massacre. The same indifference was to greet the genocide of the Jews during World War II.

This change in European societies is clearly detectable in the drawings and paintings of Otto Dix and Georg Grosz, who shattered "the silence of painters" by demonstrating the horror of war by its effects on the world to which it had given birth. The urban landscape that they depict is chaotic and ravaged, with cripples and war-wounded on every corner. Many of the men are in uniform. When not depicted as wrecks littering a decadent décor, they animate the stage as hysterical figures, jerking frenetically as if convulsed by electric shocks. The impression conveyed by this twitching tangle of forms is that of a society that is sick, fissured, racked by incessant spasms, eaten away by some cancer. Günther Anders remarked that Grosz's muse was "nausea" (*Ekel*) and the subject of his art was not the real world, but rather "the destruction of the real world." The social universe represented by Grosz knows nothing of "natural death": violent death has become its normal condition. The extermination of men and the destruction of all that surrounds them—"being killed" as "the most natural and ordinary modality of being"—that is the world as depicted by Grosz.[57]

The devaluation of human life was accompanied by the dehumanization of the enemy, an idea that was diffused by military propaganda, the press, and scholarly literature too. The Great War provided an ideal field in which to apply the racial stereotypes developed by social Darwinism and the medical sciences since the last quarter of the nineteenth century. Nationalist propaganda abandoned all rational argument on the score of causes and justifications for the conflict, and instead appealed to a sense of belonging to a community under threat, calling for total, blind allegiance. The enemy always assumed the features of a hostile "race," systematically described as "barbarian." The Entente powers accused Germany, which had introduced chemical weapons, of displaying a brutality worthy of "Huns"—the word regularly appeared on their posters. In France, Doctor Edgar Berillon explained this cruelty by characteristics specific to the German "race," characteristics not only physical (the morphology of their skulls, and the smell and toxicity of their excrement) but also moral (their servility) and psychological (their lack of self-control and their warrior fetishism), all of which clearly likened the Germans to "primitive" peoples. As he saw it, the war atrocities revealed the Germans' criminal atavism; their practices had no equivalent "except among the semi-savage peoples of central Africa and the Congo."[58] As for Germany, it responded to such accusations with irony, recalling all its Nobel prizes; it also officially urged that "in the interest of humanity and civilization, colored troops should no longer be used in the theatre of war in Europe." Its propaganda represented the world conflict as a fight to defend the people of an ancient culture against both the assault of Slavic and semibarbaric hordes in the East and the threat in the West of the multiracial Franco-British armies, which were infiltrated by savagery owing to the presence of colored soldiers and cannibals. The land of Kant and Beethoven saw itself under threat from cannibalistic tribesmen in uniform.[59]

## A LABORATORY OF FASCISM

The racist dehumanization of the enemy and the growing indifference with regard to human life also found expression in a brutalization of political life, which now adopted the language of warfare and methods of confrontation inherited from the trenches.[60] In Germany and Italy, where political institutions and civilian societies underwent an overall dislocation when the conflict was over, warfare erupted into political life through the proliferation of armed units both on the left and above all on the extreme right (ranging from the Freikorps to the SA and from the *Arditi del Popolo* to the *fasci di combattimento*). The ancient myths according to which the soldier was the embodiment of heroism and patriotism were now supplemented by the image of the "new man" forged by total warfare. Postcards and propaganda posters repeatedly depicted troops marching to battle, singing the national anthem, ready to fight with courage and a spirit of self-sacrifice. In traditional iconography, the fighter was represented as a proud human figure of classic beauty, in many cases ennobled by the medal displayed prominently on his chest that testified to his heroism. In contrast, the soldier of the new nationalist propaganda presented all the characteristics of Jünger's Worker: he was cold, mechanical, and menacing. His appearance was anything but human; his physique had a metallic, artificial quality. His hair was not visible, and his face, sculpted in clean, sharp lines, seemed to fuse with the steel of his helmet. A heavy charge of aggression and, you could say, nihilism emanated from his body, while his expression conveyed an unshakable tenacity. The Fascist ethic, one of whose symbols was the steel helmet (*Stahlhelm*), acknowledged its warlike origins.[61] At the same time, within the codes of Fascist aesthetics, this soldier who had turned his own body into a metal machine and his muscles into intermeshed steel gears that combined power with beauty could not fail to evoke the ancient warrior sealed into his armor. An ancestral aura surrounded the soldier of total modern warfare, the worker who was the embodiment of the technologized Romanticism of the Conservative revolution.[62]

The language of politics was transformed too. Italian Fascism turned war into the supreme moment of life, exalting battle as a kind of fulfillment for man and for the triumph of strength, speed, and courage. In Germany, in the wake of Ernst Jünger, who had idealized warfare as an "internal experience" (*inneres Erlebnis*),[63] Carl Schmitt interpreted it as both the condition and the triumph of politics in that it constituted a theater of confrontation between friend (*Freund*) and foe (*Feind*). He produced neither a rational explanation nor an ethical condemnation of warfare: it simply stemmed from the recognition of an "existential" conflict with the enemy, "the other, the alien," whose otherness represented "the negation of one's own form of existence."[64] The no-man's-land between the enemy trenches became the place that symbolized the new ethos of total warfare: a zone where law was suspended, where existence was affirmed by combat, a space of destruction and death, where life was exposed, naked, to the onslaught of a mechanical violence in the midst of a nature that had regressed to a wilderness thanks to the power of technology. "No-man's-land" was the concrete embodiment of Schmitt's "exceptional state" (*Ausnahmezustand*) and Martin Heidegger's "age of nihilism."[65]

In society, the war marked a decisive stage in the process of the nationalization of the masses.[66] Nationalism now became aggressive as it attempted to reproduce the logic of the front. The aesthetics of war flooded public spaces. Nationalism swung toward a crusading spirit of warfare (*Glaubenskrieg*). No longer was war exclusively the ideal of the ruling elites, but now it took hold of the masses, becoming a collective passion that was subversive and "revolutionary"; it opposed the tradition destroyed by the war and aspired to the establishment of a new order. New leaders of plebeian origin emerged from the masses, men marked by the experience of trench warfare and deeply involved in the postwar political crisis.[67] World War I had set in train a new syncretism between mythology and technology, counter establishment and political existentialism, nihilism and vitalism, Romanticism and Futurism, which was to find its most complete expression in National Socialism. In 1913, one year before the outbreak of war, the Italian writer Giovanni Papini, a strange figure who started out as an avantgarde critic but who eventually converted to nationalism, then Fascism, and ultimately conservative Catholicism, published in the periodical *Lacerba* an astonishingly prophetic essay entitled "Life Is Not Sacred." It contained a coldly lucid diagnosis of the new century, which Papini regarded as an age of industrial extermination in which life had irreparably lost its sacred aura. He wrote:

> The whole of life in our time is devoted to organizing necessary massacres, some visible, others invisible. Whoever dares to revolt in the name of life is crushed in the name of that very life. Industrial civilization, like the civilization of war, feeds on carrion. Cannon-fodder, and machine-fodder. Blood in the fields and blood in the streets; blood in the tent and blood in the factory. Life can only rise higher by so to speak discharging its ballast, a part of itself, as it moves on.[68]

This passage indicates that the horrors of modern warfare had already been foreseen, and in some cases even celebrated in advance, for example, among the Italian Futurists, by avant-

garde literary figures. The warfare of the Great War was to operate as a powerful catalyst without which the Fascist synthesis
could not have happened, or at any rate could not have taken
the forms that it did. Warfare's intrusion into politics, the nationalization of the masses, the brutalization of the language
and methods of conflict, the birth of a new generation of political militants shaped by their experiences at the front, the formation of violently nationalistic and racist movements led by
an elite of angry plebeians convinced that arms were called for
if democracy was to be replaced: all these were features of the
face of the Europe that emerged from four years of war. The
new nationalist leaders no longer despised the masses in accordance with a conservative tradition that had been followed by
figures ranging from Joseph de Maistre to Frederich Nietzsche. Like Hitler, they had discovered their vocation as charismatic leaders in the streets, in demonstrations by war veterans
and other postwar conflicts, or else, like Mussolini, in the
context of war they had undergone a metamorphosis that had
projected them from socialism into nationalism. This counterrevolution was not purely reactionary, as those of 1789 and 1848
had been, but became a "revolutionary reaction" or a "revolution against the revolution."[69] It was reactionary in its response
to the workers' movement, the Russian Revolution, and Bolshevism, but "revolutionary" in that it aspired not to restore the
past, but to create a new order that was nationalist, antidemocratic, and authoritarian. Such a convergence between populist
nationalism and anti-Marxist and reactionary National Socialism had already been detectable at the end of the nineteenth
century, in particular in France during the Dreyfus affair, but
was fully realized only after 1918. World War I was thus a decisive stage in the creation of Fascism.

In the Fascist view, well illustrated by writers such as Filippo T. Marinetti, Wyndham Lewis, and Ernst Jünger, warfare
lost its instrumental character and became an end in itself, an

existential experience that derived its source and justification from itself. For Marinetti, warfare was an aesthetic delight: he exalted its beauty, dynamism, movement, and artificial violence. Warfare realized the "dream of a metallic human body" for the first time, adorned the fields with "flaming orchids flowering from machine guns," broke the silence of nature with the symphony of cannons, and created new geometric forms with the flights of bomber aircraft and "the smoke spiraling upward from burning villages."[70] For Jünger, war was a creative experience that he described as a warrior ecstasy and an eruption of sensuality. He depicted battle as "an orgy of fury" in which the refined pleasures of civilization and the intellectual sophistications of urban culture gave way to the "sonorous clashing of a reborn barbarity." The energy that emanated from soldiers' bodies was that of a fairy-tale festival, a pagan ritual that resuscitated a primordial, unadulterated violence with the power to reestablish a cosmic harmony that *Zivilisation* had destroyed: "As acrobats of death, masters of flames and explosives, splendid wild beasts, they hurtled across the trenches. At the moment of impact, they were the quintessence of all the warrior aggression that the world has ever produced, an exacerbated amalgam of bodies, will, and senses."[71] For Jünger, this frenzy created by the means of destruction of modern warfare was "comparable only to the forces of nature" that assimilated man "to a howling storm, a furious sea, and rumbling thunder."[72] The eroticism of the warrior community, technological nihilism, and antihumanism were the essential ingredients of a new philosophy of death in which extermination became an end in itself. This new vision of death and destruction marked an anthropological turning point in the process of civilization, and prepared the way for the genocides of the twentieth century.

Walter Benjamin, who was a reader and sharp critic of Jünger, discerned in this philosophy of warfare the expression of an *aestheticization of politics* that found its fullest form in Fascism. This exaltation of the unleashing of elements celebrated technology not as a "key of happiness" but as a "fetish of decadence." It idealized battle, destruction, and death as an intensely lived primordial experience (*Urerlebnis*), a kind of electric shock and spasm that breaks the continuum of experience (*Erfahrung*) that is transmitted and crystallized in culture. Through its aesthetic transformation of the landscape, warfare produced the illusion of an artificial recreation of an original aura lost at the time of industrial capitalism. But this "dark, runic magic" resulted only in widening the gap between society and nature, in a rite of destruction and death.[73] In *One Way Street* (*Einbahnstrasse*), Benjamin wrote: "Masses of human beings, gases, and electric forces were hurled across the flattened countryside. High frequency currents crossed the landscape, new stars rose in the sky, the air and the depths of the sea hummed with the sound of propellers, and sacrificial ditches were hollowed out in Mother Earth." The description ended by commenting on the new face of humanity that modern warfare had revealed: "During the last war's nights of extermination, a sensation comparable to an epileptic fit shook the entrails of humanity."[74] In "The Weapons of Tomorrow" ("Die Waffen von Morgen"), an astonishingly prophetic article written in 1925, Benjamin alludes with cold irony to the chemical weapons that the German chemistry combine I. G. Farben was producing, weapons that contained the secrets of new techniques of murder.[75]

Let me try to sum up. The Great War was a major historical turning point that marked the advent of the twentieth century, for it constituted at once a moment that condensed the preceding century's metamorphoses of violence and also the cataclysmic beginning of "the age of extremes," with all its new practices of extermination. The Taylorist army integrated the principles of authority, hierarchy, and discipline. and the instrumental rationality of modern industrial society and provided a foretaste of the forms of domination founded on the mobilization of the masses that were to climax under the Fascist regimes. The camps for prisoners of war were a crucial link in the transition from the panoptic model of the disciplinary prison to the world of the concentration camps of the totalitarian regimes. Once warfare was industrialized, the dehumanization of the enemy and his carefully planned destruction took a decisive leap forward, without which the Nazi practices of extermination would have been hard to imagine. Total warfare tended to efface all distinctions between the military and civilians—as is most clearly shown by the deportation and internment of the civilian populations of the occupied territories and nationals of enemy countries—and this revealed the link between warfare and genocides, which was to become a typical feature of the twentieth century. The genocide of the Armenians was thus both a product of the lacerating contradictions inherent in the archaic Ottoman state and a result of total warfare. The war constituted a laboratory for new forms of propaganda from which the Fascist regimes learned a great deal—propaganda designed not only to dehumanize but also, in many cases, to racialize the enemy. The focus that propaganda directed upon a number of racial stereotypes such as the innate barbarity of the "Boches" and, even more significantly, the "cannibalism" of the black troops serving in Anglo-French armies is equally revealing. On the one hand, it underlined the link between the mental world of colonialism and that of total warfare; on the other, it afforded a glimpse of the central place that racism was to occupy twenty years later, in the conception and practices of the Nazi war waged in order to conquer Lebensraum. The condensation of all these aspects in the experience of the Great War made it both a point of rupture in the history of Europe and an anteroom of National Socialism.

# 4

# *Classification and Repression*

## "JEWISH BOLSHEVISM"

"A s the carriers of Bolshevism and intellectual leaders [*geistige Führer*] of the Communist idea, the Jews are our mortal enemy. They are to be annihilated [*Sie sind zu vernichten*]."[1] This directive, communicated to the Wehrmacht soldiers in Minsk on October 19, 1941, during the German advance into the Soviet Union, used a formula that Nazi propaganda hammered home throughout the war. It would be easy to multiply examples of such orders, which exalted the war against "Jewish Bolshevism" as "a struggle for the existence [*Daseinkampf*] of the German people and a defence of European culture against the Asiatic and Muscovite flood (*Überschwemmung*)."[2] Hitler used exactly the same language in his private conversations. In 1941 he justified the war on the Eastern Front by the need to exterminate the "hotbed of plague [*Pestherd*]" that the Jews represented. As he saw it, this was the only way to restore the unity of Europe.[3]

The myth of "Jewish Bolshevism" had been widely disseminated after World War I, when it became the slogan of the counterrevolution in Germany, Hungary, and Russia. The vision of Bolshevism as a kind of virus, a contagious disease the bacilli of which were the revolutionary Jews of central and eastern Europe, who were rootless and cosmopolitan and lurked unseen in the anonymous metropolises of the modern industrialized world, hostile to the very idea of nation and traditional order, was extremely common in conservative culture. The spectre of "Jewish Bolshevism" haunted the nightmares of the ruling elites, liberal and nationalist alike, confronted by the revolutionary uprisings of 1917–21. In Russia, the White Terror set out to "neutralize the Jewish microbe" and launched against "Jewish Bolshevism a propaganda campaign whose violence," the historian Peter Kenz tells us, "prefigured the Nazi propaganda of World War II."[4] The Jewish presence lurking behind Russian Communism was strongly denounced in Rome, by the publication *La civiltà cattolica (The Catholic Community)*[5] and also in France, by the right-wing press. In 1920, Charles Maurras, writing in *Action Française,* declared that "the appalling vermin of Jews from the East" that had infested a number of Parisian districts (*arrondissements*) were bringing in "fleas, pestilence and typhus, while waiting for the revolution."[6]

Many manifestations of this myth are to be found in the literature and propaganda of the period, including those emanating from figures and institutions that, two decades later, were to become irreducible opponents of the Nazi regime. *The Protocols of the Learned Elders of Zion* was fabricated in the mid-1890s by order of Piotr Rachkowsky, the chief of the Paris office of the Okhrana, the czarist secret police. Translated into many languages after World War I, it became an international best-seller.[7] In Britain, which, unlike the countries of central Europe, remained unaffected by the revolutionary wave, the historian Nesta Webster pondered upon the causes of the worldwide revolution, and explained them by the existence of a "Jewish conspiracy" designed to overturn civilization.[8] In May 1920, *The Times* of London published an article, "The Jewish

Peril," in which it proposed an enquiry to investigate the veracity of the *Protocols*. One month later it represented Trotsky as
the leader of a Jewish Internationale aiming to conquer the entire planet.[9] Winston Churchill designated Marx, Trotsky, Bela
Kun, Rosa Luxemburg, and Emma Goldman as the incarnation of "a world plot that aims to topple civilization." In a passage that is reminiscent of the *Protocols,* Churchill detected in
the Jewish presence "the force hidden behind every subversive
movement of the nineteenth century." He then went on to
paint an alarming picture of the existing crisis: "Today, this collection of extraordinary figures from the lowest levels of the
great towns of Europe and America has grasped the Russian
people by the collar and virtually made itself the uncontested
master of a huge empire."[10] As he saw it, the Bolshevists were
"enemies of the human race," "vampires sucking the blood of
their victims," and "atrocious baboons in the midst of ruined
towns and heaps of corpses." At their head was Lenin, "a ram-
pant monster atop a pyramid of skulls," surrounded by a "vile
group of cosmopolitan fanatics." It was an image closely evoca-
tive of an anti-Semitic poster that represented Trotsky as a Jewish ogre enthroned upon a mountain of skulls.[11]

In Germany, the Nazi vision of the Soviet Union as the
monstrous result of an alliance between the Jewish intelligentsia and the Slavic *Untermenschen* had been prefigured by
Thomas Mann in his 1918 diary entries; Mann was the writer
who, twenty years later, would represent the tradition of the
*Aufklärung* (Enlightenment) in exile. It is true that his language
was literary, not biological, and his argument stemmed more
from the romantic view of the intellectual conflict between
culture and civilization (embodied a few years later by the
opposed figures of Naphta and Settembrini in *The Magic
Mountain*) than from the stereotypes of fin-de-siècle racial anthropology. But the fact remains that he did interpret the Russian revolution as the result of the convergence of the Jewish

intelligentsia and Slavic nihilism. He saw it as "an explosive mixture of Jewish intellectual radicalism and Slavic Christian mysticism" and warned against the diffusion of such an epidemic: "A world that preserves even an atom of the instinct of self-preservation must take action against these people with all the mobilizable energy and promptitude of martial law."[12] In 1919, that energy was to be deployed by the army of Gustav Noske and the Freikorps. In Germany, Hungary, and Poland, anti-Communist posters provided a strongly expressive illustration of counterrevolutionary imaginary representations. In these, Bolshevism assumed the features of horrible imaginary Semitic monsters, spectres of death that symbolized imminent catastrophe—a horde of savage beasts that were the very incarnation of brutal, barbaric violence. In the Baltic states, which were plunged into civil warfare between 1918 and 1920, the struggle against "Jewish Bolshevism" was one of the main pillars of counterrevolutionary agitation, and the Freikorps's recruiting among the German minorities there played a leading part. Estonia, Latvia, and Lithuania constituted a laboratory for the amalgamation of "race" and "class" that, twenty years later, was to be central to the Nazi war against the USSR. A number of future Nazi leaders proved themselves there, among them Alfred Rosenberg, the theorist of biological racism who later became the Third Reich's minister for the eastern territories. He was born in Tallinn, Estonia, but settled in Munich at the end of 1918, after witnessing the civil war in his home country.[13]

By the early 1920s, the vision of the Jew as the motivating force of the revolution and the master of the Russian empire was one of the bases upon which the Nazi ideology rested. Ernst Nolte simplifies greatly when he reduces National Socialism simply to a product of the Russian Revolution, but undeniably the revolution was a major dimension of it.[14] The Jewish presence within Bolshevism—and within other revolutionary movements in central Europe—may well have been particularly striking, but all the same it was not October 1917 that engendered Nazi anti-Semitism. Anti-Bolshevism was grafted upon a German nationalism whose principal bases had always been anti-Semitism and pan-Germanism. The amalgamation of those three elements—anti-Communism, imperialist expansionism, and anti-Semitic racism—was the distinguishing feature of Nazism and bestowed upon it a radicalism previously unknown. The novelty of Nazism—apart from the fact that its "energetic measures" far exceeded anything Thomas Mann or Churchill could have desired or conceived at the end of World War I—lay in its extreme biologization of anti-Semitism, which reformulated the myth of a "plot" and the old cliché of the Jew as an antinationalist element in terms of racial hygiene. Hitler, who inherited this portion of his views from *völkisch* nationalism, regarded the Jews as a virus that had to be eradicated, of which Bolshevism was simply an external political manifestation. From 1920 onward, his speeches were full of references to Marxism as a Jewish creation, to Communism as a "racial tuberculosis,"[15] to the Jews as "carriers of Bolshevism," and to Communist parties as "the mercenary troops" of the Jews. Eberhard Jäckel has drawn up an impressive list of the characterizations of the Jews to be found in *Mein Kampf.* Almost all are borrowed from the vocabulary of parasitology: "The Jew is a worm in a rotting body, a pestilence worse than the black death of the past, a carrier of bacilli of the worst kind, the eternal schizomycete of humanity, the spider that slowly sucks out a people's life-blood through its pores, a band of rats that fight each other to the death, the parasite within the bodies of other peoples, the very epitome of a parasite, a scrounger that proliferates more and more, like a harmful bacillus, the eternal leach, the vampire of all peoples."[16] Alfred Rosenberg, who had denounced Bolshevism in the early 1920s in a pamphlet titled *Plague in Russia (Pest in*

*Russland*), was to declare twenty years later in *The Myth of the Twentieth Century,* that the accession of Lenin and Trotsky to power in 1917 had only been possible "within the body of a people diseased both racially and psychologically."[17] In *Mein Kampf,* Hitler famously alluded to the tragedies that Germany could have avoided if only the Jews had been wiped out by gas in the course of the war.[18]

The Nazis' predilection for pathological images is certainly well illustrated by their extensive use of the notion of "Jewish Bolshevism" as a manifestation of the sickness of the social body.[19] Hitler's favorite medical metaphor besides syphilis and tuberculosis was cancer, against which the Third Reich had adopted the most radical and far-reaching hygienic policy in Europe.[20] Meanwhile, this contamination of political propaganda by medical and epidemiological language was matched by a massive adoption of political metaphors on the part of scientists. Bernhard Fischer-Wasels, one of the founders of research into tumors, described the embryonic stage of cancer as "a new race of cells" quite distinct from others, and he proposed therapy aimed at the destruction of this pathological race [*Zerstörung der pathologischen Zellrasse*]." Researchers called cancerous cells "anarchists," "Bolsheviks," and "breeding grounds of chaos and revolt." Other specialists favored expressions like "revolutionary cells" (Hans Auler) or "a state within a state" (Curt Thomalla). The historian of science Robert N. Proctor concludes that at this time the language of medicine was permeated through and through by political ideology.[21]

## CLASS RACISM

While the convergence of counterrevolutionary feeling and anti-Semitism may have forged a new category, "Jewish Bolshevism," that became a peculiarity of the National Socialist ideology, the definition of the class enemy in terms of race, the vision of political revolt as expressing a sickness in the social body, and the stigmatization of the revolutionary as a carrier of a contagious virus were phenomena that dated from much earlier. A telling example is provided by France at the beginning of the Third Republic, with its mixture of positivism, scientism, racism, and conservatism, radicalized by the memory of the political uprisings of 1848 and 1871. The almost parallel rise between 1860 and 1890 of new disciplines such as microbiology (Louis Pasteur), experimental medicine (Claude Bernard), anthropology (Paul Broca, Paul Topinard), eugenics and racial anthropology (Georges Vacher de Lapouge), criminal anthropology (Lacassagne), neurology (Jean-Martin Charcot), crowd psychology (Gustave Le Bon, Tarde), and sociology (Emile Durkheim) created conditions that favored an amalgamation of science and politics that then found expression in a biological approach to social behavior and in a kind of medicalization of the strategies of power.[22] Phenomena as diverse as syphilis, alcoholism, prostitution, hysteria, criminality, insubordination to the new social hierarchies, strikes, and insurrections were thus considered to be multiple expressions of one and the same sickness within the social body, or even as hereditary flaws, pathogenic centers that found in urban and industrial society their most favorable breeding grounds. The cholera epidemics, still vividly remembered at this time, had been deeply upsetting to bourgeois sensibilities, undermining the self-confidence of the ruling classes and their faith in progress within a prosperous, pacific, heirarchized, and ordered society. Cholera was immediately associated with an external menace imported from the East or from Africa and originating among "uncivilized" peoples and carried by migrants, then passed on by the (social and biological) lower classes, whose insalubrious living quarters became centers of infection. Cholera soon came to be regarded as a form of social subversion.[23] Similarly, the Communists were seen as recidivist criminals, the carriers of an epidemic that had to be countered by radical measures. Since the contagion threatened to affect parts of society that were still healthy or curable, the pathogenic agent, the virus made up of a hard core of "born criminals" who were both dangerous and incurable, needed to be totally eliminated. The state set itself up as a biopower, called upon to intervene in society just as a surgeon operates when called upon to amputate the gangrenous part of an infected organism.[24]

This "social biologism," a description that Sartre applied to French literature in the period following the Commune, had its roots in the Industrial Revolution period, when the working classes were "racialized" and physically separated from the privileged strata. It was then that social inequality as manifested by disease began to be perceived as expressing the physical and moral degeneration of the proletariat.[25] And it was then that the state began to elaborate hygienist public policies designed to isolate the "dangerous classes" spatially, just as cholera patients were isolated in hospitals. This view of society was grafted upon another imaginary representation, which had been inherited from the counterrevolution and preserved by liberal culture, whose language it now recycled. On the one hand, it exhumed the old cliché that branded revolt an eruption of ancestral and barbaric violence, a threat to civilization that surfaced from deep within it, a relic of the primitive horde that had survived on the margins of the civilized world and now reemerged into the light of day (the murderous masses of Burke's *Reflections on the Revolution in France* and the "Vandals and Goths" of Tocqueville's *Souvenirs*.[26] On the other hand, within the context of imperialism, this primitive barbarity was identified with that of the "savages" of the colonial world. The figures of the proletarian insurgent, the criminal, the hysteric, the prostitute, the savage, and the wild beast now became interchangeable. The class enemy was not recognized as a legitimate political opponent, but was "racialized" and animalized. De facto political repression was represented, and justified, as wiping out a body that was alien to civilization, as a measure of public hygiene. The contamination of politics by biological and scientific discourse had direct implications for political and military therapies designed to preserve order. "Race" was used as a metaphor to designate a class that was feared, a class whose threatening otherness was apprehended in biological, physical, psychological, and moral terms, the better to set it at a distance and if necessary to crush it.[27]

The designation of the laboring classes as an "inferior race" became a commonplace of European culture in the age of triumphant industrial capitalism. Around the mid-nineteenth century, the English essayist Henry Meyhew described the poor of large towns as "wandering tribes in the midst of civilized society," tribes with all the characteristics of primitive peoples. They were recognizable both from their physical appearance, with their "high cheekbones and jutting jaws," and from the way they spoke their incomprehensible jargon. They were lazy, refractory to the discipline of work, uncouth, violent, filthy, and lacking any sense of propriety or religion. In an 1883 enquiry into urban poverty, George Sims evoked the colonial image of a "dark continent" right there in the midst of civilization. A number of anthropometric studies were hastily undertaken to confirm these observations and hypotheses.[28] In the figure of the sailor—uncouth and restless, and frequently suspected of cannibalism, in accordance with a widespread myth—the right-thinking press had detected one living link between the savages of the extra-European world and the primitive races, that is to say the laboring classes, of the civilized world.[29]

In France, "class racism" was to find its theorists, at the turn of the century, in Gustave Le Bon (1841–1931) and Georges Vacher de Lapouge (1854–1936), the former one of the founders of crowd psychology, the latter the founder of "anthropo-sociology." In his 1894 work, *Lois psychologiques de l'évolution des peuples (The Psychology of Peoples),* Le Bon produced a "psychological classification of the human races," attributing to each a "mental constitution" along with its physical and anatomical traits. His analysis led him to detect a substantial similarity between the "inferior races" and the lower classes. The latter were the "savages" of the civilized world, which they threatened from within, like some kind of survival of barbarism. "The lowest levels of European societies resemble primitive beings," he wrote.[30] In his view, the distance separating the ruling elites and the urban proletariat was "as great as that separating the white man from the negro."[31] Needless to say, political democracy and egalitarianism were chiefly to blame for civilization's regression toward barbarity, a recognition encouraged as much by immigration as by the class struggle. Vacher de Lapouge was soon transcribing Le Bon's thesis in the terms of eugenics: the idea of a biological origin for social inequalities and of their immutable and hereditary nature runs through all his works from 1880 right through to the interwar period.[32]

The repression of the Paris Commune of 1871, which according to different estimates produced in a single week between 10,000 and 30,000 victims, provides a particularly illuminating illustration of the tendency to racialize the class conflict. The historian Robert Tombs has shown that the Versailles Army, the force that put down the revolt, was composed of neither fanatical Bonapartists nor peasants and provincials seeking revenge against a detested and demonized capital. The dominant feeling among the troops was not that they were repressing a political revolt but rather that they were extinguishing a criminal fire in a town that had fallen into the hands of the "dangerous classes." Tombs stresses that, seen this way, the counterrevolution took on a foundational character: "It stemmed from the idea, borrowed from social biology and destined for a dire future, that society was threatened by the 'degeneracy' of its 'lower' elements."[33] Although marked by episodes of blind, unbridled violence, like any civil war, this military repression was essentially strictly planned, disciplined, organized, cold, and impersonal. Most of its victims were not killed in the streets but were arrested, escorted to sorting centers, judged, and executed. Those operations were all kept entirely separate and entrusted to different military units, so that very few soldiers could really gain a clear idea of the extent of the carnage. One of the consequences of the methods of this repression was that those who carried it out did no more than obey orders and were exonerated of any ethical responsibility. Tombs recognized in this repression a forerunner of the bureaucratic, impersonal genocides perpetrated by "ordinary men" of more modern times.[34] The authorities also deported many communards to the prisons of New Caledonia, in accordance with the old custom of isolating carriers of contagious diseases in leper colonies and lazarets and the more recent practice of imposing quarantines in order to control the spread of cholera.[35]

Political repression seen as a disinfection of the social body presupposed the dehumanization of the enemy, who was demoted to the level of an animal or an inferior biological species. The most inspired expression of an interpretation of the Commune in zoological terms is to be found in an article written by Théophile Gautier in October 1871. Here is a by now classic extract from it:

In all major towns there are lion-pits, heavily barred caverns, designed to contain wild beasts, stinking animals, venomous creatures, all the refractory perversities that civilization has been unable to tame, those who love blood, those who are as amused by arson as by fireworks, those for whom theft is a delight, those for whom rape represents love, all those with the hearts of monsters, all those with deformed souls; a disgusting population, unknown in the light of day, pullulating in sinister fashion in the depths of subterranean darkness. One day it happens that a careless jailer leaves his keys in the doors of this menagerie, and the wild beasts rampage with savage roars through the horrified town. Out of the open cages leap the hyenas of '93 and the gorillas of the Commune.[36]

Ernest Feydeau's words echo Gautier's: "It is not barbarity that threatens us now, not even savagery that is let loose among us, but bestiality pure and simple."[37] Zola, a writer who described society with the scientific rigor of a doctor, was more sober and measured. He saw the Commune as a flare-up of "fever" (a theme dear to Burke), a delirium caused by the alcohol that had taken hold of the people of Paris and that had to be halted. The bloodbath in which the Commune was drowned was simply "a horrible necessity." In *La Débâcle,* he described the Commune as "a growing epidemic, chronic befuddlement, a legacy from the first siege, aggravated by the second," which had fallen upon "a population without bread, but with spirits and wine in barrelfuls" and which "had steeped itself in drink and now went crazy on the smallest drop."[38] The novel ends with a naturalistic metaphor that looks forward to the regeneration of society after the catastrophe, as to "a sure renewal of eternal nature" and as "a tree throwing up a strong, new shoot after the dead branch, whose poisonous sap had yellowed the leaves, had been cut away."[39]

In *Les Origines de la France contemporaine (The Origins of Contemporary France)*, the first volume of which appeared in 1878, Hippolyte Taine sketched a picture of the French Revolution that provides, with extraordinary feeling, a review of all the stereotypes of a conservative France still traumatized by the memory of the Commune. A number of familiar themes recur: *Zoology:* The Revolution opened Taine's eyes to "the animal instinct of revolt."[40] The revolutionary was an individual who had gone off the rails, who had risen up from the depths beneath civilization to destroy it—"a barbarian or, worse still, a primitive animal, a grimacing, bloodthirsty and lascivious monkey that kills with sneering laughter and cavorts over the destruction that it has produced."[41] *Race:* He compared the masses in action to "rampaging Negroes" suddenly attempting to "steer the vessel that they had seized."[42] *Barbaric regression:* "The most profound observer of the Revolution will find it comparable only to the invasion of the Roman Empire in the fourth century," except that now the Huns, Vandals, and Goths come neither from the North nor from the Black Sea—"They are in our midst."[43] *Disease:* the Jacobins had "sick minds" and Marat was "mad"; the insurgents were inflamed by a contagious virus, like people who become feverish from "contact with those suffering from fever."[44] The virus that had first made its appearance in 1789 had been transmitted from one generation to the next, right down to the epidemic of 1871. Ten years after the Commune, Taine described it as "a pathological germ which, having penetrated the blood of a suffering and seriously sick society, produced fever, delirium, and revolutionary convulsions."[45]

The Commune provided strong motivation for the earliest works on crowd psychology by Scipio Sighele and Gustave Le Bon. At the time of Charcot and his studies on magnetism, the crowd, a typical example of the aggregation of polarized atoms, was analyzed as an urban pathology, the visible manifestation of a social structure eaten away by cancer and already rotten. The crowd was hysterical, feminine, irrational, violent, subversive. For Maxime du Camp, the Commune crowds were composed of a monstrous gathering of the sick: pyromaniacs, individuals "affected by homicidal monomania" or "violent lycanthropy," prostitutes, and alcoholics. Then he added, "Virtually all those unfortunates who fought for the Commune were what alienism terms 'sick.' "[46] In the early 1890s, his diagnosis was confirmed by Gabriel Tarde, one of the foremost figures in sociology and criminal anthropology. His explanation of crowd psychology was based on the law of imitation, and he defined the masses' actions as a bestial and primitive regression. He declared that the crowd was a modern phenomenon which, at the heart of civilized peoples, constituted the reappearance of an "impulsive and maniacal beast, played upon by its mechanical instincts and habits, sometimes even an animal of the lower orders, an invertebrate, a monstrous worm in which the senses are diffused and which continues to move in uncoordinated movements when it is decapitated."[47]

Cesare Lombroso (1835–1909), the main representative of Italian positivism, sanctioned the exorcism of the revolution at the heart of a Europe haunted by the spectre of the Commune on "scientific" grounds. As Daniel Pick has underlined, to Lombroso, criminality constituted a kind of biohistorical anachronism: the criminal was an individual whose psychological development had been arrested and in whom it was consequently easy to detect pathological tendencies by means of a careful anthropometric analysis.[48] In the wake of Lombroso, the theory of criminal atavism immediately attracted lively interest within the scientific community: it was ascribed to crossbreeding, which was seen as the principal cause for the reappearance of primitive behavior in the civilized world. Expressions such as "defilement" and "the atavism of crossbreeding" were much bandied about in this connection.[49] Arthur Bordier, a professor at the Paris School of Anthropology, made a study of murderers who, as he saw it, presented characteristics "peculiar to prehistoric races" that had "disappeared among present-day races" but which "recur in them through a kind of atavism." He then explained, "Understood in this way, the criminal is an anachronism, a savage in a civilized land, a kind of monster, something like an animal which, born from parents long since domesticated, tamed, and accustomed to work, suddenly appears with all the untameable savagery of its earliest ancestors."[50]

Criminal anthropology thus placed itself at the service of social prophylaxy, intent upon spotting delinquents and protecting society from criminal atavism and anarchy. As Lombroso saw it, rebels suffered from hereditary diseases that were potentially contagious and were easily detectable from physical anomalies. In *The Criminal Man* (*L'uomo delinquente,* 1876), he produced a detailed list of the morphological characteristics of the "born criminal"; black, frizzy hair; an aquiline or hooked nose; heavy jaw; large, protruding ears; a flat skull; jutting brows; huge zygomas; a "shifty" air; in many cases a squint; a pale face; bloodshot eyes.[51] In this portrait, which reflects all the imagery of the fin-de-siécle criminal, it is easy to pick out a number of physical elements that at that time were already being attributed to Jews and that a few years later were to mold the archetype of the Bolshevik armed to the teeth. The iconography and caricatures of the anti-Semitic press were saturated with this imagery, the diffusion of which peaked in the interwar period. The born criminal was a monster, a degenerate. In this category, Lombroso classified the regicides and terrorists of 1793, the Communards, and the anarchists. Having examined the files of forty-one anarchists in the archives of the anthropometric service of the Paris Prefecture of Police (the famous Bertillon archives), this anthropologist from Turin concluded that 31 percent of them possessed all the characteristics of the typical criminal. In another inquiry, he analyzed fifty photographs of Communards and discerned the criminal type in 12 percent of them. These constituted the kernel of the epidemic, he decided. Once that infectious hotbed was eliminated, society would be able to proceed successfully with the reeducation of the rest, the criminals with "acquired organic defects."[52] Lombroso, who regarded himself as a social reformer and enlight-

ened scholar, drew a distinction between revolution (a "psychological phenomenon") and revolt (a "pathological phenomenon"), reckoning that the former stemmed from social
contradictions and injustices and could therefore be justified,
while the latter were linked with criminal deviance. In his
work *Political Crimes and Revolution,* he classified the Commune among the revolts that had been provoked by the harmful action of "born criminals." [53]

The analysis of revolutionary crowds elaborated at the end
of the nineteenth century by Scipio Sighele and Gustave Le
Bon bore the stamp of Lombroso's influence. In *The Criminal
Crowd* (1891), Sighele borrowed the most inspired of Taine's
words to describe the revolution as a metamorphosis in which
the people were transformed into "a wild beast" moved by "a
ferocious and bloodthirsty instinct." He pondered the causes of
such a mutation that suddenly turned "a people of laborers and
honest workers" into "a monster of perversity," and immediately came up with the key to the puzzle: the presence of a contagious agent. When revolutions occur, he declared, the people
become "corrupted" by agitators who in normal times remain
hidden in the darkest depths of society—madmen, degenerates, alcoholics, criminals, "repellent people" (*gente schifosa*)—
but now unexpectedly surface like mud from the bottom of a
pond.[54] Gustave Le Bon favored the thesis of criminal atavism.
In his *Psychology of Crowds* (1895), he regarded revolutions as a
historical regression, a "return to barbarity," the manifestation
of a "repetitive syndrome" that, if not stifled at the outset,
would certainly threaten to plunge France back into the Terror
of 1793.[55]

Le Bon's social Darwinism and Vacher de Lapouge's eugenics certainly influenced the formation of the elitist theories of
Gaetano Mosca, Vilfredo Pareto, and Robert Michels.[56] Mosca
was an antidemocratic conservative, Michels was later to join
the Italian Fascists, and Pareto would always be regarded by

Mussolini as one of the ideological precursors of his own regime. Mosca and Pareto criticized the most extreme formulae of Vacher de Lapouge and Otto Ammon (meanwhile expressing admiration for Taine, however), but they produced theories to explain the lower classes' objective incapacity to emancipate themselves or to assume any historical function other than that of "a leaderless mass" destined to be mobilized by the "aristocracies" that were permanently engaged in a struggle for power that involved the never-ending "alternation of elite groups."[57] Social Darwinism and eugenics were key milestones along the tortuous path that was to lead Robert Michels (1876–1936) from socialism to Fascism. Along with Weber's analysis of the administration, these constituted the underlying source for his famous 1911 study, *Political Parties: A Sociological Study of the Oligarchical Tendencies of Modern Democracy.* On the basis of a brilliant analysis of the process of the bureaucratization of German social democracy, he produced a theory of the "iron law of oligarchy," which, he posited, was the ineluctable destiny of any mass political party.[58] In other words, the proletariat was doomed to remain the prisoner of a hierarchical and stratified system. It would never be capable of organizing itself, emancipating itself, or controlling its representatives in a democratic fashion. This explains the highly complimentary remarks about Gustave Le Bon that Michels makes in his book.[59] In 1912, after breaking with German social democracy, Michels defended his thesis, the origins of which were to be found in social Darwinism, that the lower classes were physically and biologically inferior, which he claimed his own research confirmed at the sociological level.[60] Social Darwinism, anthropological pessimism, and political elitism all converged to produce both the conclusion that social inequalities were a law of nature and a radical rejection of democracy, which was now considered to be either a sociological impossibility or an illusion that ignored the deep-seated nature of the masses.

## THE NAZI SYNTHESIS

Was there a link between the rise of this "class racism" and the birth of modern anti-Semitism, which was no longer religious but racial? The perception of social and political revolt through the categories of racial anthropology and criminology was contemporary with the then swiftly mutating stereotypes of hatred against the Jews but was in the main *separate* from them. At the end of the nineteenth century, Jean-Martin Charcot's studies on hysteria were being used not only by criminal anthropology, for the classification of delinquents and striking workers, but also by many scholars who were anxious to find a scientific explanation for the "Jewish character." The vision of hysteria as a Jewish syndrome, first put forward by Charcot, was soon widely accepted in the medical sciences.[61] Hysteria, neurosis, psychic frailty, physical deformity, precarious health, and epilepsy came to be regarded as typically Jewish traits. At the Salpêtrière hospital, Henry Meige claimed to have discovered the key to interpret the myth of the "wandering Jew," which he identified as a literary transfiguration of the Jewish syndrome of the "traveling neuropath."[62] Léon Bouveret, a disciple of Charcot, described neurasthenia as a hereditary illness particularly prevalent among Jews and Slavic peoples.[63] Others regarded this as the source either of the "Jewish genius" or else of the Jews' physical and intellectual degeneration. Anti-Semitism drew heavily on this eclectic reservoir of clichés on the Jewish "anthropological type." An example that leaps to mind is the physical portrait of the Jew in Edouard Drumont's *La France juive* (*Jewish France*), in which a hooked nose and neurosis are accompanied by more archaic features such as a *fetor judaico,* or Jewish stench.[64] But this tendency to racialize the "Jewish type" was by no means confined to anti-Semites. The Catholic Dreyfusard Anatole Leroy-Beaulieu was inclined to recognize the existence of the Jewish genius, but nev-

ertheless underlined the flaws, both psychic and physical, of the
Jews as a race:

> Their physical strength and muscular vigour has diminished
> from one generation to the next. Their blood has become im-
> poverished, their stature has shrunk. Their shoulders and
> chests are narrower. Many Jews from large centers of Jewry
> have an etiolated and stunted look. Many of them manifest a
> kind of racial bastardization and degeneration.

Needless to say, he goes on to claim that "all too often, that
physical degeneration is matched by moral degradation."[65] For
Ignaz Zollschans, an Austrian Zionist doctor, and for Max
Nordau, the foremost theorist of degeneration at the turn of the
century, the purpose of the creation of a Jewish state was precisely to halt the process of racial degradation among European
Jews.[66] In Palestine, a new, vigorous "muscular Jewishness"
(*Muskeljudentum*) would take the place of the malingering,
neurotic Jewish intellectual, already gnawed away by the sickness of the large cities of the West.

The "racialization" of Jewish otherness ran parallel to that
of social and political subversion, but the two remained
distinct. Anti-Semitism, particularly in a country such as
France—at least up until the Dreyfus affair—was part and
parcel of the cultural baggage of both the Socialist left and the
antirepublican right. That kind of anti-Semitism, the ideological expression of an immature form of anticapitalism—what
August Bebel had called "the socialism of fools"—could not be
condensed in the figure of the Jewish revolutionary, which was
not often to be found in France, the land of emancipation,
where a solid layer of "state Jews" (*juifs d'état*), Jewish state
functionaries, had developed.[67] The fusion of these stereotypes
in the image of "Jewish Bolshevism" was a product of the 1917
revolution in Russia and the German and Hungarian revolu-

tions of 1918–19. The conjunction of the two previously separate sets of stereotypes—the one cultural, the other racial—resulted from the leading role that Jewish figures played in those uprisings: for example, the charismatic figures of Leon Trotsky, Yakov Sverdlov, Grigori Zinoviev, and Karl Radek in Russia; Rosa Luxemburg, Paul Levi, Ernst Toller, Gustav Landauer, and Kurt Elsner in Germany; and Bela Kun in Hungary. After 1917, the hysteric, the born criminal, and the wild, bloodthirsty beast of the Commune assumed the features of the Jewish revolutionary. This resulted in both the anti-Semitic language of the counterrevolution (the above-mentioned examples of Churchill and Thomas Mann represent the nobler end of the spectrum here) and, on the other, the far more radical racialization and biologization of revolutionary movements by Nazi propaganda. Once the infectious hotbed of revolution—the "Jewish bacillus" to which Hitler so often referred—had been detected, it was felt that repression alone would be inadequate to restore lasting order unless it included a racial purge, for only this could eradicate the evil at its source. Thus, even after the defeat of the workers' movement and the process of forcing German society to "fall into step" in 1933, the task was still not completed. That is why, in 1941, in the war against the USSR, the destruction of Communism, and the extermination of the Jews were conceived to be absolutely indissociable tasks. The advance of the Wehrmacht into Poland, Lithuania, Ukraine, Russia, and the Baltic states was followed by the operations of the *Einsatzgruppen,* or "mobile special units," charged with the systematic massacre of Jews and the political commissars of the Red Army (800,000 Jews and 600,000 political commissars were eliminated in the first year of the conflict).[68]

Only in Germany was anti-Semitism a central characteristic of fascism, for there the figure of the revolutionary Jew was particularly visible. Neither in Italy in 1922–25 nor in Spain at the time of the civil war did Mussolini or Franco resort to it, unlike in Germany where, right from the start, anti-Semitism was one of the pillars of the counterrevolution and later the National Socialist movement. Anti-Semitism was a peculiarity of Nazism and was linked with the historical context, both political and cultural, in which the latter had evolved. The war, together with the revolutions of 1917–19, certainly acted as a catalyst, but that peculiarity stemmed from the synthesis between a racial approach to Jewish otherness and a biologization of political subversion, both elements that had been discernable in several European countries in the second half of the nineteenth century but had never come together before. The racial approach to Jewish otherness was part of the whole positivist and science-oriented culture of western Europe; the biologization of political subversion had found its most influential ideologues and propagandists in France, at the time of the Commune, at the beginning of the Third Republic. Thus, although Nazism certainly manifested traits that were typical of the German context, in its fusion of anti-Bolshevism and anti-Semitism, and counterrevolution and racial extermination, it certainly was a European product.

## EXCURSUS ON "RACIAL HYGIENE"

The first stage in the biologico-racial extermination carried out by Nazism was the "T4 Operation," the euthanasia of the mentally ill and certain other categories of handicapped people. It was set in train at the beginning of the war but was halted (or at least reduced) in 1941, because of the protests from the churches, but not before it had claimed over 90,000 victims.[69] The elimination of these human beings was part and parcel of the same project for the racial remodeling of Europe that led to the massacres of the *Einsatzgruppen* and to the death camps. On a strictly technical level, the euthanasia of the mentally ill constituted the laboratory of the genocide of the Jews, since it was in the course of the T4 Operation that the system of extermination by gas, which was to be developed on a vaster scale in the death camps, was first tried out. Some of the medical and administrative staff involved in the initial trials of this method of murder were later transferred to Auschwitz, to apply their skills there. Raul Hilberg has described this "psychiatric holocaust" as the "prefiguration, at once conceptual, technical, and administrative, of the 'Final Solution.' " [70]

Although euthanasia as a means of social prophylaxis remained a specific feature of Nazi biopolitics without equivalent in twentieth-century history, it was rooted deep in a culture that was part of Europe and the Western world as a whole. Racial anthropology and eugenics were disciplines that had been well established in all Western universities, particularly in the Anglo-Saxon world and the Scandinavian countries, ever since the late nineteenth century. A policy of enforced sterilization for the mentally ill had been adopted in the United States, first in the state of Indiana, in 1907, then, between 1909 and 1913, in California, North Dakota, Wisconsin, Kansas, Iowa, Nevada, and Washington. [71] During the 1920s, similar methods were applied in Switzerland, Sweden, Norway, and Denmark, and frequently by governments led by Social Democratic parties. In 1899, the American scholar W. Duncan McKim published *Heredity and Human Progress,* in which he proposed euthanasia not only as a way to procure "a sweet death" for beings suffering from incurable diseases, but as a process of "artificial selection" of the population, with a view to "improving the human race." [72] The Nazis greatly admired *The Passing of the Great Race* (1916), a work by the American eugenicist Madison Grant, and had been publishing translations of it ever since 1925. [73] In 1910, the "Civilization" article in the *Encyclopedia Britannica* declared that the future of humanity would probably be ruled by "the biological improvement of the race, thanks to the application of the laws of heredity."[74] This article was eliminated in 1945, but it had testified not only to the legitimacy enjoyed by eugenicist theories within the scientific community but also to their broad dissemination among the Anglo-Saxon public.

Social Darwinism and eugenics justified the war as an instrument of racial selection. For the German eugenicist Otto Ammon, the war assured "the superior nations with energy and intelligence the supremacy that they deserved." He compared the army to "a huge sponge" that at the moment of mobilization would absorb all men able to bear arms and, after a short war, would operate "a selection of the most skillful, the most vigorous, and the most resistant of them."[75] In 1897, Lord Wolseley opened the London Philosophical Society Congress with a speech titled "War and Civilization" in which he represented warfare as a means of getting the best elements of humanity to triumph.[76] In 1911, on the eve of World War I, the British military specialist Sir Reginald Clare Hart set out an ambitious biological theory of warfare according to which, in opposition to the naïve pacifism of Comte and Spencer, he saw in war an instrument of progress and an essential opportunity for the regeneration of humanity that was indispensable for the reestablishment of a demographic equilibrium between nations. In his conclusion, Hart pleaded for "an implacable war for the extermination of the beings of inferior nations."[77] An echo of these debates can be found within Italian Futurism, which in its first manifesto in 1909 hailed warfare as "the only hygiene for the world."[78] One of the first (rare) critics of social Darwinism, the French man Jacques Novicow, seized acutely on the political ends of this doctrine, which considered "collective homicide to be the cause of progress for humankind."[79]

Even in Italy and France, where the Catholic church opposed any policy of enforced sterilization, the theories of eugenicists had been widely disseminated, although less so than in the Anglo-Saxon world. The social Darwinism introduced by

Cesare Lombroso toward the end of the nineteenth century had paved the way for it. The first Italian congress on "social eugenics" took place in Milan in 1924. Five hundred doctors took part and discussed topics such as the "rational cultivation of mankind" (*viricultura razionale*) and "biological improvement of the race" (*biofilassi*).[80] Mussolini's regime initially favored racism that was "spiritualist-Roman" rather than "biologico-Aryan," but it was certainly in the name of "racial hygiene" that the racial and anti-Semitic laws of 1938 were promulgated, following the Ethiopian War and the alliance with Nazi Germany.[81] In France—where writers from Zola to Barrès had by and large been promoting eugenicist themes and ideas of "degeneration"—the principal propagandist for eugenics was still Georges Vacher de Lapouge, who in *L'Aryen, son role social* (1890) proposed a campaign of mass sterilization in order to forestall the chaos and barbarity of democratic and egalitarian modern societies. The "natural selection" described by social Darwinism, which defended a laissez-faire policy and liberal capitalism, seemed to him to be no longer at all effective in the Western world, which had by now created its own mechanisms of immunity. It was therefore necessary to adopt a eugenicist policy of planned racial selection, the only way to avoid the massive elimination of inept people that would one day become necessary if the existing dominant trend was not halted. In his *Les Sélections sociales* (1896), he set out the main lines of a project to promote the use of artificial insemination in order to produce a new kind of human being, who would be superior both aesthetically and intellectually. "Zootechnical and scientific reproduction would be substituted for spontaneous, bestial reproduction," he announced.[82] In 1935, shortly before his death, Vacher de Lapouge acknowledged that Hitlerism was a pan-Germanist caricature of his ideas.[83] Although doctors who favored "negative" eugenics—a policy of enforced sterilization or even euthanasia—were in the minority, they included some important figures, among them the Nobel Prize winners Charles Richet and Alexis Carrel. In 1919, Richet published *Les Sélections humaines,* chapter 20 of which was entirely devoted to "the elimination of abnormals." [84] In *Man, the Unknown* (1935), Carrel proposed the creation of an "establishment for euthanasia, equipped with the appropriate gas," which would make it possible to resolve the problem posed by abnormals "in a humane and economical fashion." [85] In 1904 Carrel settled in the United States, where he worked at the Rockefeller Foundation and elaborated a kind of synthesis between French Fascism and American eugenics. In 1941, he returned to France, where he became the director of the French Foundation for the Study of Human Problems, set up by the Vichy regime (where, as Carrel explained, the absence of the word "race" in the name of the organization was "for psychological reasons"). It was at this time that he started to envisage the advent of a "biocracy." [86]

In Germany, eugenics fell on particularly fertile soil. Already in the late nineteenth century, a number of anthropologists, ranging from Ernst Haekel to Ludwig Wolfmann, had proposed euthanasia as a social therapy, in an early synthesis of eugenics and Nordic racism. In 1905, in Berlin, the doctor Alfred Ploetz founded the Society for Racial Hygiene (*Gesellschaft für Rassenhygiene*), which used a number of scholarly journals to disseminate its principles. In 1927, under the Weimar Republic, eugenics received an important boost from the creation of the Kaiser Wilhelm Institute for Anthropology, Human Genetics, and Eugenics, which centralized research and elaborated the first plans for the sterilization of the mentally ill, criminals, and "morally retarded" individuals. At first the institute tried to remain strictly scientific, as can be seen from its decision to favor scholarly terminology (*Eugenetik*) for concepts with ideological connotations such as *Rassenhygiene*. [87] But from 1930 on it began to seek a synthesis between eugenicist theories and *völkisch*

thought, and some of its members adopted an openly racist attitude.[88] In fact, during the thirties doctors were one of the most
Nazified professional categories in Germany.[89] The passage of
a law on enforced sterilization in 1933 encountered very little
resistance.[90] Doctors certainly played their part in developing a
family-planning policy that relegated women to the role of "re-
producers of the race," under the control of the political authorities; the corollary to this was a campaign for enforced
sterilization.[91] Of course, it would be incorrect to equate eugenics with Nazi racial biology. The policy of sterilization in the
United States and the Scandinavian countries without a doubt
stemmed from an ethically unacceptable social prophylaxis, but
it was not openly contaminated by the racist ideology that, for
example, led the Nazis to decide in 1934 on the enforced sterilization of the "Rhineland bastards," the children of mixed race
born from the unions of black soldiers and German women
during the period of the French occupation of the Ruhr.[92] Similarly, a considerable gap separates the sterilizations carried out
in the United States and the extermination of handicapped
people implemented by the Nazis during World War II. However, while such equations should definitely be avoided, we
should at the same time be aware of the links between the Nazi
technico-scientific massacres and the eugenicist culture with
racist connotations that was for decades widely disseminated
by many doctors, psychiatrists, anthropologists, ethnologists,
and biologists in important positions in the universities and
scientific institutions of Europe and the United States. The eugenics and "racial hygiene" that provided Nazism with a number of essential bases for its vision of the world were part of
Western culture, were solidly implanted in its liberal institutions, and found enthusiastic representatives among scholars
and intellectuals at many levels (nationalists, liberals, conservatives, and even socialists). This was the tradition from which

National Socialism drew the "scientific language" with which it reformulated its anti-Semitism: the Jews were assimilated to a "virus" that generated "diseases," and their extermination was assimilated to a measure of "cleansing" and an operation of "prophylaxis."

Throughout the thirties, the international scientific community refused to take Nazi propaganda seriously. The organic link between "race hygiene" and the Nuremberg Laws did not seem to pose an obstacle to scientific collaboration between German eugenicists and their Anglo-Saxon colleagues. In 1936, when the Nazi regime had already promulgated those laws and carried out several tens of thousands of enforced sterilizations, the University of Heidelberg bestowed an honorary doctorate upon Professor Harry Laughlin, one of the most highly reputed of the American selectionists, who was the director of the Center for Eugenicist Research at the laboratory at Cold Spring Harbor, New York. In his speech of thanks, he declared that he was honored by such recognition and considered it "proof that German and American scientists understood eugenics in the same way."[93] This episode seems to confirm the view of the historian Daniel Pick, that it would be easy to find "the equivalent of Nazi discourse on race, eugenics, and degeneration" in both England and the United States during the interwar period.[94] André Pichot goes further: "Hitler did not invent much. Most of the time he was content to take up ideas that were already in the air and to carry them to their ultimate conclusion. Euthanasia and profound meditations on 'lives that did not deserve to be lived' were commonplaces at that time."[95] Horrified condemnation of the Nazi crimes and the eugenicist theories that had inspired them was only voiced *post factum.*[96] Until the end of the war, Nazi eugenics was considered neither inhumane nor aberrant, nor even—despite the massive emigration of Jewish scientists—prejudicial to collaboration in the domain of research. The unanimous condemnation of Nazism after 1945 masks those former good relations. There was no equivalent to Mengele in the Anglo-Saxon world, but his practices were simply an extreme development from an ideology that was firmly rooted in Western culture as a whole.

# 5

# *Extermination:*
# *Nazi Anti-Semitism*

## THE JEW AS AN ABSTRACTION

The image of the Jew as the incarnation of an abstract and impersonal modernity permeates the whole of Western culture from the mid-nineteenth century onward. The diffusion of this image affected the continent as a whole, but particularly the countries where the Jews were most numerous and their socioeconomic integration and cultural assimilation penetrated most deeply. To some extent Jews came to symbolize an urban and industrial modernity perceived as entailing a loss of traditional values and heralding an anonymous, cold, rational, alienating world that was, in the last analysis, inhuman. The earliest socialists, particularly in France, frequently equated anticapitalism and anti-Semitism, while the conservatives held the Jews responsible for the disappearance of a "natural" order founded upon tradition, in which aristocratic values were perpetuated without hindrance, an integral part of a hierarchical society. The ghettos had disappeared early on in the democratization of the Old World, when cleavages of caste and rank were tending to be replaced by the uniform and impersonal equality conferred by the status of citizen. The emancipated Jews had constructed their success upon the basis of this modern, mechanical, and soulless society, which truly was the antithesis of the preindustrial organic and natural "community." They were seen as representing the abstract, economic rationality of finance and democratic universalism, tailored to fit an equally abstract kind of humanity that was defined by the law instead of by tradition, a sense of belonging, and deep local roots. In this conflict that irreducibly set "community" (*Gemeinschaft*) in opposition to "society" (*Gesellschaft*), the Jews were perceived as a chemically pure concentrate of the latter. The real Jews were replaced by the universal and undifferentiated category of "the Jew." The mutation that had liberated Jews from their former status of pariahs and had "normalized" them within society, where they became citizens "like everyone else" and, at least subjectively, equal members of a national community, was accompanied by a new form of negative "otherness." The age-old stranger living on the margins of society was still a stranger because he now embodied a modernity that itself had become strange and hostile to a nation still strongly attached to its traditional values. As the personification of the abstraction that dominated the social relations of the capitalist, urban, and industrial world, the Jew was stripped of his real features and became simply a metaphor for modernity.

The above view was not expressed only as political anti-Semitism. It also found expression in a vast philosophical, economic, and historical literature in most Western countries. In his *Philosophy of Money* (1900), Georg Simmel—himself for many years a victim of anti-Semitic discrimination in the German academic world—drew attention to a whole series of affinities between Jews and monetary circulation, modern "intellectualism," and liberalism. After emphasizing the Jews' ability to "move more freely within the combinations of formal logic than in creative production concerned with its own content,"[1] he suggested that, as "totally uprooted" human beings, they were the representatives of a society dominated by the abstract rationality of money: "Money, because it comes between things and man, allows the latter a *quasi* abstract existence, free from any direct regard for things."[2]

In France at the turn of the century, the vision of the Jew as a pure abstraction was widespread just as much among Dreyfusards as among nationalists and the anti-Semitic. In the eyes of Maurice Barrès, the Jew was an incomparable logician: whose "reasoning [was] as incisive and impersonal as a bank-account."[3] The Catholic Dreyfusard intellectual Anatole Leroy-Beaulieu regarded the Jew as a "pensive figure," an individual "characterized by the predominance of the nervous system over the muscular system,"[4] frequently neurotic or even hysterical and far more inclined to physical deformity than an Englishman or a native of the Auvergne: "It would be ridiculous to expect a Jew to have the fine body of a Greek or the fine presence of an Englishman."[5] This tendency to "physical degeneration" was, however, balanced by an impressive, calculating rationality: "The Jewish mind is a precision instrument; it possesses all the accuracy of a weighing machine."[6] For André Gide, Jewish intelligence was "marvelously organized, organizing, clear-cut, and classificatory," capable of picking up the trail of an idea and reconnecting the thread of an argument just as one arranges objects in a drawer. But rational rigor had a downside: the Jew possessed "the most anti-poetic of minds,"[7] (a view that later also surfaces in Sartre's *Anti-Semite and Jew*).[8]

When reformulated in anti-Semitic literature, this view gave rise to the antithetical pair Jew/Aryan. Edouard Drumont, in his work *La France juive,* was one of the first to contrast the commercial, cerebral, and calculating "Israelite" with the agricultural, heroic, and creative "Aryan."[9] This work was already amalgamating and interweaving nationalism, racism, and anti-Semitism. It drew on a remarkable mixture of themes borrowed from French socialist anti-Semitism (Proudhon and Toussenel), Catholic and reactionary anti-Judaism (Bonald and Barruel), and the new scientific racism. *La France juive* did not yet go so far as to propose a coherent and well-defined "therapy," but it did present a number of affinities with German *völkisch* anti-Semitism.[10] During the interwar period, several writers placed the Jew/Aryan antithesis at the center of their works. Céline, in his *Bagatelles pour un massacre* (*Trifles for a Massacre,* 1937), depicted the Jewish intellectual as a "literate robot," totally bereft of any creative spirit and fundamentally a corrupter of art. Nothing was more alien to the Jew than "authentic, spontaneous emotion, geared to the natural elements," for his deep-seated vocation impelled him to seek out "whatever was standard in all things"; hence the dominant role that he played in society, for "a modern civilization means total standardization, body and soul, under the Jew."[11] Pierre Drieu la Rochelle devoted one of his best-known novels, *Gilles* (1939), to this theme. In it he produced an ironic formulation to convey the abstract and profoundly inauthentic Jewish existence: "A Jew is as horrible as a polytechnician or a product of the Ecole Normale."[12]

In Germany, the Jew/Aryan dichotomy corresponded to the conflict between *Zivilisation* and *Kultur* and left its mark on the writings of all the theorists of the "Conservative revolution." In his most famous book, *The Decline of the West* (1918), Oswald Spengler opposed the "wisdom" (*Weisheit*) typical of premodern societies, permeated by religious spirituality and the foundation of *Kultur,* to the abstract "intelligence" of the industrial and urban world, which smacked of atheism (*Intelligenz klingt atheistisch*) and was the basis of modern, rational, but rootless *Zivilisation.* Wisdom presupposed an organic, natural community, in which order stemmed from religion and myths. The intelligence that was flourishing in the anonymous and cosmopolitan metropolises had replaced religion and myth with "scientific theories." The opposition between those two worlds explained why the Jews were totally alien to *Kultur:* "The Jew has never understood the internality of the Gothic, the castle, and the cathedral; and the Christian has understood neither the superior, almost cynical intelligence nor the 'financial thinking' [*Gelddenken*] at which the Jews excel." [13]

The economist Werner Sombart was to reformulate the opposition between *Kultur* and *Zivilisation* in several of his works, in which it took on the form of a conflict sometimes between "the artist" and "the bourgeois," sometimes between "heroic peoples" (*Heldenvölker*) and "commercial peoples" (*Händlervölker*), and ultimately between Germans and Jews. [14] In 1911, he had written *The Jews and Economic Life* (*Die Juden und das Wirtschaftsleben*), designed to challenge Weber's thesis of an "elective affinity" between the Protestant ethic and the spirit of capitalism and to defend the view that modern capitalism was a Jewish creation. In Weber's view, capitalism was founded upon a stable system of production and the rational pursuit of profit capable of renewing itself, two phenomena that had received a powerful boost from the Reformation. In opposition to this, Sombart set his vision of capitalism as a market economy in which the realization of profit was detached from all ethical constraints. Capitalism implied a rational organization of production, the division of labor, international trading, financial investment, and a stock exchange; its development produced large towns, a society of masses, and the universal reification of existence, and favored impersonal relations between people. "Rationalism is the fundamental characteristic of both Judaism and capitalism," Sombart declared. [15] All this provoked an irreparable break with the organic totality of *Kultur,* shattered the fullness of life enjoyed by peoples rooted in the land and tradition, destroyed "the intuitive imagination of the artist," and engendered the specialists of industrial civilization—mutilated men (*Teilmenschen*), with limited, unilateral minds, cut

off from nature and reduced to executing mechanical and de-
meaning tasks. Capitalism had sent the artist packing in order
to make way for the bourgeois, with his "utilitarian teleology"
(*Zweckbedachtheit*), his calculating mind, his "moral mobility"
(*moralische Beweglichkeit*), and his abstract intellectualism.[16]
This rationalization of life matched the Jewish psyche, which
had always been accustomed to the abstraction of monetary circulation. So the rise of capitalism and the bourgeois civilization
coincided with the jewification of the world. The whole of society now conformed with the abstract and calculating rationality of the Jew. Once the "heroic peoples" were dethroned by
Jewish modernity, the whole of culture would be irremediably
destroyed and corrupted. Abstract rationalism would per-
meate the arts and literature. According to Sombart, an illuminating example of this tendency was provided by Max
Liebermann, the famous Jewish painter and director of the
Berlin Academy, who "painted with his brain."[17] This anti-
Semitism steeped in romantic anticapitalism reflected a deep
cultural pessimism that, for Spengler in particular, made
modernity seem to represent a "decline" comparable to the fall
of the Roman Empire. He formulated this diagnosis using naturalistic metaphors in which the decadence of culture corresponded to the aging of man or the withering of nature in the
winter.

This rapid overview sketches in the cultural background to
the new anti-Semitism, which, between the last quarter of the
nineteenth century and World War I in Europe, replaced or
came to overlay the traditional anti-Judaism, with its religious
origins, and then became an integral part of European culture
in the interwar period. Far from being confined purely to Germany, this new perception of Jewry was also widespread in
France, which at the turn of the century was a veritable hotbed
of anti-Semitic nationalism. As Ze'ev Sternhell has emphasized, "Drumont and Wilhelm Marr, Jules Guérin and the

marquis de Morès, Adolf Stöcker and the Austrian Georg von Schönerer, Vacher de Lapouge and Otto Ammon, Paul Déroulède and Ernst Hasse, the leader of the Pan-German League, resemble each other as closely as twins." [18]

The Anglo-Saxon world was less deeply affected by this new kind of anti-Semitism but was certainly not free of it, as is clear from a number of significant English literary figures ranging from Dickens, who in *Oliver Twist* gives Fagin the characteristics of the calculating Jew, to Kipling and Chesterton, for whom the Jew, midway between the black and the white man, was already a figure with racial connotations. [19] But it was in the writings of the inventor of the factory assembly line that Anglo-Saxon anti-Semitism found its true manifesto. In *International Jew* (1922), Henry Ford contrasted "Jewish financiers" to Anglo-Saxon "captains of industry," figures who embodied two different modalities of existence: being in order to "make" versus being in order to "get," to have. The pursuit of profit was "vicious, anti-social, and destructive" among Jews, but "legitimate and constructive" among "WASP" bosses. [20]

Modern anti-Semitism took various forms, and evidenced different nuances, depending on its representatives, but it was founded upon the opposition between "community" and "society," according to the classic definition by the German sociologist Ferdinand Tönnies (1855–1936). This kind of modern anti-Semitism may be expressed by a binary schema, summarized as follows:

| COMMUNITY | SOCIETY |
| --- | --- |
| Aryans | Jews |
| spirit | abstract reason |
| agriculture | industry |
| aristocracy | bourgeoisie |
| the soil | rootlessness |
| country | town |

| | |
|---|---|
| honor | a utilitarian ethic |
| quality | quantity |
| concrete | abstract |
| wisdom | intellectualism |
| religion | science |
| myths, metaphysics | calculating rationalism |
| community | individualism |
| people | masses |
| creation | standardization |
| hero | merchant |
| nation | citizenship |
| nationalism | cosmopolitanism |
| traditional values | abstract universalism |

The Aryan/Jew dichotomy constituted one of the pillars of nationalist culture, acting as a permanent factor in the construction and negative stigmatization of the otherness in opposition to which a national identity was forged. The Dreyfus affair was a moment of paroxysm in this process. Before the 1914 war, Germany undoubtedly was one of the foremost localities affected by this modern anti-Semitism, especially at the intellectual level, but it was certainly not unique in the European context. It was only in the postwar period that the elements of this continentwide cultural magma crystallized into the anti-Semitism *sui generis* that constituted the ideological bedrock of first the Nazi movement, then the Nazi regime.

## A REGENERATIVE VIOLENCE

World War I was apprehended in Germany as an unmissable opportunity to halt the advance of *Zivilisation* and assert the rights of a *Kultur* capable of resisting, renewing itself, and proving that the "heroic" spirit could wipe out the (American and English) "mercantile" spirit and the (French) universalist spirit, both of which were represented by a cosmopolitan Jewry, fundamentally alien to the very notion of a fatherland—*Helden* (heroes) opposed to *Händler* (tradesmen), the "ideas of 1914" opposed to the "ideas of 1789". The clash between the frame of mind in which Germany threw itself into the war and the reality of this modern military conflict—in which the heroic spirit of the fighter was obliged to give way to a preplanned confrontation between rationalized armies—was bound to transform the critique of modernity described above. The war was the moment when, for many intellectuals, *Kultur* became reconciled to modern technology. These intellectuals now abandoned their passive contemplation of decadence, switched to active revolt against *Zivilisation,* and became capable of confronting *Zivilisation* on its own terms and fighting it by its own means. Cultural pessimism turned into "reactionary modernism,"[21] and the neoromantic critique of capitalism became a "conservative revolution." Nostalgia for the traditional community was converted into a utopian aspiration toward a new community, a *Volksgemeinschaft* of the future. The Weimar Republic was overturned not in order to restore the Prussian Empire, but to create a Third Reich. As we have seen, Ernst Jünger, in several of his books written in the twenties, had devoted himself to an aesthetic celebration of warfare seen as the source of a virile meeting of man with nature. The product of that meeting was the "worker" (*Arbeiter*), a figure forged in the trenches of the Great War who, as Jünger saw it, was the embodiment of the rebirth of the German soul, a rebirth characterized by authoritarian, military, and technological order.[22] The Jew, needless to say, was the perfect antithesis to this "worker." In 1930, Jünger devoted an essay to a critique of the *Zivilisationsjude* (civilization Jew), whom he branded "a son of liberalism" and a body alien to the German nation, within which he acted as a destructive agent.[23] Anti-Semitism was an indispenable agent in this metamorphosis from cultural pessimism into reactionary modernism. It was thanks to the metaphorical figure of the Jew—not necessarily defined in biological terms by Jünger—that cultural antimodernism fused with technical modernity, and anti-Enlightenment feeling was reconciled to the technico-industrial world. Capitalism was now seen as creative, on condition that it was linked with the *Volk,* was "Aryanized," and became the instrument of a national community. The industrial bourgeoisie with Aryan blood and rooted in Germanic soil became creative and reintegrated *Kultur,* in contrast to the Jewish bourgeoisie, which was branded parasitic, mercantile, and cosmopolitan.

Under the Weimar Republic, the traditional image of the Jew as the representative of abstract universalism became the target of an aggressive, vengeful nationalism, radicalized by defeat and the humiliation of Versailles. For the geographer Karl Haushofer, this was the starting point for renewed reflection on the concept of *Lebensraum.* He criticized modern geopolitics, which he regarded as a limited discipline "alien to the soil," and opposed the abstract political entity of the state, with its frontiers fixed by international law, to the concrete reality of the *Volk.* He conceived the state as a living, biologically determined organism, whose territorial dimensions should not be established by law but should be fashioned by the vital energy of its people.[24] In other words, the state frontiers should now delimit not a juridicially defined space, but an "ethnic ground" (*Volksboden*), the product of "a will for living space (*lebendige Raumwille*), which expressed an organic process that he compared to the blood of a living being flowing over and through the old national borders (*Grenzdurchblutung*).[25] The Jew, as the representative of abstract rationality, served Haushofer as a negative illustration of his *völkisch* concept of space. His writings did not relate to real Jews, only to "whatever is Jewish" (*das Jüdische*), an adjective used as a noun that he associated with modernity in general: liberalism, socialism, communism, law, democracy, universal suffrage, international commerce, large towns, and so forth.[26]

After 1933, Carl Schmitt, the roots of whose anti-Semitism were not racial but essentially cultural, also contributed to the construction of a conceptual system of total domination.[27] He began by reformulating his political philosophy in anti-Semitic terms. He now considered the Jews to be the carriers of "normative thinking" (*Gesetzesdenken*), anchored in concepts of "legality" (*Legalität*) and equality (*Gleichheit*) and alien to the "legitimacy" (*Legitimität*) and the "homogeneity" (*Gleichartigkeit*) upon which the National Socialist state was founded. Schmitt declared: "There are people who live without land, without state and without church, solely within the 'law'; normative thought is the only kind that they consider to be rational; all other kinds, in contrast, seem to them incomprehensible, fantastical, and ridiculous."[28] To him the end of Kaiser Wilhelm's empire in 1918 meant that a "concrete" political order, based on monarchical institutions, was being replaced by the "domination of the law" (*Herrschaft des Gesetzes*) and by an abstract and rootless democracy in which "the law lords make the king their subject" (*Die Herren der Lex unterwerfen den Rex*).[29] Under Weimar, nothing remained of the concrete political order embodied by the monarchy. He considered the republic to be a democratic system paralyzed by the arguments and chaos of a spineless pluralism. The Jews, as representatives of normativity and abstract, deterritorialized juridical rationalism, had played a key role in the "dissolution" of the old imperial order (and it was, of course, a Jewish jurist, Hugo Preuss, who was responsible for drawing up the Weimar constitution). At the center of the "concrete" political order that had been restored under the National Socialist regime was not an abstract and formal "law" (*Gesetz*), but *Nomos,* meaning, according to his interpretation of Greek etymology, a norm conceived as a process of organizing political forms and space that could not be reduced simply to institutions.[30]

In 1936, Schmitt headed a congress of Third Reich jurists that was designed to condemn the sinister and corrupting influence of the "Jewish spirit" (*jüdischer Geist*) on German law. He urged its representatives to liberate the latter from all its liberal encrustations and to reestablish an organic anchorage at the heart of the *Volk*. He associated the figure of the Jew with all the (to his mind) negative aspects of modernity, just as Haushofer did. Therefore, in his writings the "Jew" became a simple metaphor. For example, Schmitt referred to the Austrian philosopher of law, Hans Kelsen, as "the Jew Kelsen," adding that "the mere use of the word 'Jew' gives rise to a salutary exorcism."[31] In 1938, in an essay on Hobbes, he reaffirmed his identification of the Jews with the liberal tradition and represented modern constitutionalism as a Jewish creation, the work of a long line of writers stretching from Spinoza through Moses Mendelssohn to Friedrich Julius Stahl.[32] Between 1937 and the outbreak of World War II, Schmitt devoted a number of texts to theorizing on a "total war" that would sound the knell of international law and in which traditional notions of *jus ad bellum* (the right to initiate war) and *jus in bello* (the law during war) would lose all meaning, making way for the destruction of the definitive "enemy" (or, in Jünger's existentialist terms, "the Other"). The conclusion that he drew from this analysis is summed up in a vision of warfare—the modern war of extermination—as a practice of extermination that implemented a policy.[33] At the time of the German occupation of Czechoslovakia in April 1939, Schmitt wrote an article on the irreconcilable opposition between the German notion of *Grossraum,* the "large space" of German domination, and international law, which he linked with a "universalism" of Jewish origin.[34] In the 1941 essay "Peoples' Large-Space Order" (*"Völkerrechtliche Gross-*

*raumordnung")*, he insisted that the notion of *Grossraum* should not be understood literally, simply as a compound of the terms "large" and "space." He interpretated the expression not purely quantitatively but also *qualitatively* and linked it with the concept of *Lebensraum* elaborated by Ratzel at the beginning of the century: a "creative" (*schöpferische*) space.[35] The concept had to be given a concrete content—"land, soil"—that had very little to do with the "empty spaces" and "linear frontiers" postulated by the liberal concepts of geography and law. Those concepts were inevitably represented the most coherently by the Jews, whose rootlessness was reflected in a specific modality of political existence. "The relation of a people to the soil [that is] formed (*gestalten*) by its own establishment there and its own labor of cultivation—soil that is the source of its concrete forms of power—is incomprehensible to the Jewish mind."[36] In short, the *Grossraum* of Schmitt's vision was of an eminently existentialist nature: it implied space seen as a "conquest" linked with a vital need. "The mastery of a space (*Raumbewältigung*) is the mark of all existence," he wrote, again quoting Ratzel.[37] The mission of National Socialism was to set up a German empire founded upon this "combination of concrete order (*Ordnung*) and localization (*Ortung*)."[38] *Jus terrendi* (the power to dominate territory by force), German, versus *Jus scriptum* (written law), Jewish: Schmitt's earthy *nomos* related to a people rooted in its soil.[39]

Others were reformulating the new anti-Semitism in scientific terms. In the universities, Nazi scholars elaborated a "German physics" (*deutsche Physik*), whose main target was Einstein's theory of relativity, branded as "Jewish science." For Philip Lenard, the main characteristic of such a theory was its "abolition of the ether," so that physics was explained by means of abstract equations, instead of intuitively self-evident (*anschaulich*) images of nature.[40] Johannes Stark stressed the great difference between "Jewish" science, which was dogmatic and deductive, and a pragmatic and inductive "Nordic" science, which was linked with experience.[41]

Nazi anti-Communism followed the same logic of rejecting abstraction and biologizing otherness: the Jews constituted the brains of the Communist movement, and internationalism was a new form of abstract universalism and cosmopolitanism, which were destructive of the Aryan *Volksgemeinschaft*. Revolutionary, "countryless" Jewish figures such as Rosa Luxemburg, Karl Radek, Gregory Zinoviev, and Leon Trotsky embodied the rootless and groundless (*bodenlos*) universalism of Marxist culture.[42] For Hitler, Jews and Marxism were synonymous terms.[43] One of the first public actions of the new regime, in 1933, was the burning of Jewish, Marxist, and anti-Fascist books in the principal towns of Germany. The most important auto-da-fé, in Berlin, was presided over by Joseph Goebbels, who solemnly announced the end of "the era of Jewish intellectualism" before a crowd of students gathered outside Humboldt University.[44]

In short, one of the fundamental characteristics of Nazism was its destruction of (Jewish) abstract legal forms by a "concrete scheme of thought" (*koncretes Ordnungsdenken*), oriented by the notions of soil, race, "living space," will, and so on.[45] The old dichotomy between *Zivilisation* and *Kultur* could now be reformulated:

| ZIVILISATION | KULTUR |
|---|---|
| Judaism (*Judentum*) | Germanness (*Deutschtum*) |
| state | empire (*Reich*) |
| law (*Gesetz*) | norms (*Nomos*) |
| contract | Germanic loyalty |
| equality | hierarchy, "homogeneity" |
| legality | legitimacy |
| universalism | the people (*Volk*) |
| international law | Large Space (*Grossraum*) |

| | |
|---|---|
| humanity | nature |
| citizenship | ancestral values |
| French Revolution | historic rights |
| world revolution | Third Reich |
| Communism | *Volksgemeinschaft* |
| democracy | authority |
| pluralism | decision |
| Territory | "living space" (*Lebensraum*) |
| "Jewish mind" | Nazi *Weltanschauung* |
| abstraction | experience |
| dogmatism | pragmatism |
| "Jewish" science | "Nordic" science |

Nazism thus took over the image of the Jew as a pure abstraction and a metaphor for *Zivilisation*. In this respect, it was the offspring of nineteenth-century anti-Semitism. *Mein Kampf* is stuffed with formulae borrowed from anti-Semitic literature that attribute a Jewish character to all manifestations of political modernity. However, the specific features of Nazism—which accentuated and went beyond both traditional racist nationalism and the "conservative revolution"—stemmed from its extreme *biologization* of anti-Semitism.[46] The crusading spirit of the old religious anti-Judaism was combined with the coldness of "scientific" anti-Semitism, hence the horrifying World War II mixture of pogroms and industrial extermination, eruptions of brute violence and administrative massacre. The revolt against the "decadence" of the modern world appropriated the means of that very modernity—industry, science, technology—so as to efface any figure who might be supposed to be responsible. The negative goals of Nazism—antiliberalism, anti-Bolshevism, and counter-Enlightenment feeling—converged with its "constructive" undertakings—the racial state, the conquest of "vital space"—to produce a unified anti-Jewish crusade. The battle was waged using the juridical instruments of the state (the Nuremberg Laws), the destructive force of an army (the war of annihilation against the USSR), and the modern means of industry (concentration and extermination camps), but its necessity was explained using arguments borrowed from science. In 1942, Hitler declared, "Tracking down the Jewish virus is one of the greatest revolutions ever achieved in the world. The battle that we are waging is of the same nature as that waged in the last century by Pasteur and Koch. How many diseases originate in the Jewish virus!"[47]

Mysticism founded on nature, antihumanist irrationality, and the redemptive myth of a return to the land (through conquest) led to a policy of genocide represented as a disinfection, a purification—in short, an "ecological" measure. The Jews, who embodied an abstract (exterritorial, anational) form of humanity, were to be wiped out in the name of the preservation of nature.[48] Their elimination was necessary for the accomplishment of a natural law that presupposed a homogeneous human race. In 1941, the ideologue Theodor Seibert explained in an article in the *Völkischer Beobachter* (*People's Observer*) that the struggle against the USSR and Jewish-Bolshevism had nothing to do with the war being waged in the west against France and Great Britain, for it was a fight against an "enemy of life."[49] His thesis contained all the elements of a *regenerative* anti-Semitism.[50] In 1939, Hans Kohn had written:

> The racial theory, as evolved by the National Socialists, amounts to a new naturalistic religion for which the German people are the *corpus mysticum* and the army the priesthood. The new faith of biological determinism, fundamentally opposed to all transcendent and humanist religion, bestows upon the people an immense strength in their permanent total war against every other conception of man, be it Christian or rational. The people now represent the Reich, the realm of salvation; the enemy represents the "anti-Reich" [*Gegenreich*]; it

becomes as much of a mystical and mythical fiction as the Reich itself; only that the one is invested with all imaginable virtues, and the other with all imaginable, and sometimes unimaginable, vices. One of the weaknesses of this position lies in the fact that, whereas the Reich has a constant factor, the anti-Reich is a variable factor, according to circumstances, the political exigencies of one moment generating another adversary than those of another moment. Here Chancellor Hitler made a master move by pointing out the Jews as the anti-Reich, and by identifying all his enemies with Judaism. Thus he could "unmask" the accidental enemy of the hour, Russia and communism, Great Britain and Democracy, France and the United States, President Roosevelt and capitalism, in short, whoever seemed to stand in a concrete situation in the way of the fulfillment of German wishes, as an instrument of the devil, opposing the march towards the salvation of the Reich.[51]

This racial concept of politics, to be brought to bear directly on the *species,* not on a world inhabited by people defined as political beings, could very well (following Foucault) be described as *biopolitical,* for its aim was the management of bodies, of natural life.[52] In the terms of political science, such a concept of nature is totalitarian, for it presupposes the suppression of politics as a field of conflict and pluralism, as a public sphere superior to and emancipated from the biological sphere. Hitler considered himself the prophet of this National Socialist religion of nature, and it was certainly in prophetic terms that, in January 1939, he announced the annihilation of the Jews of Europe in the event of a new world war.[53] To the extent that anti-Semitic violence took on the aspect of a liberating crusade that aimed to fulfill the eschatological expectations of National Socialism, the latter could well be defined as a "political religion"—according to Raymond Aron, a doctrine that takes possession of people by "filling the place of a vanished faith" and by situating "the salvation of humanity here below in the distant future, in the form of a social order yet to be created."[54] Nazism was a "political religion" whose premise was a radical rejection of the Enlightenment and all humanist philosophies of secularization. However, the "regenerative" anti-Semitism of Nazism cannot be reduced to the fulfillment of Christian Judeophobia, in a predetermined drama in which Nazism undertakes the final assault against the Antichrist. A number of elements from the Christian religion were incorporated into the Nazi *Weltanschauung,* which thus possessed a syncretic character[55] in which eschatological attitudes inherited from Christianity (apocalypse, redemption, millenarianism) were intermingled with other components that were eminently modern and profane, at once scientific (purification being understood in terms of racial biology, selection, and eugenics) and also political (the conquest of *Lebensraum,* the annihilation of Bolshevism). The amalgamation of these elements produced something radically new, something unprecedented in relation to all previous forms of an ideological codification of racial and anti-Semitic hatred.

If the Jew embodied the abstraction of the modern world, the biologization of anti-Semitism was the key to a modern revolt against modernity. If the Jews were seen as a personification of the abstract social relations of capitalism, the struggle against the latter could be won by the elimination of these Jews. If *Zivilisation* meant money, finance, calculation, exchange, the stock exchange, anonymous towns, egalitarian and rootless universalism, a collection of values of which the figure of the Jew appeared to constitute the synthesis and "biologically" pure crystallization—then it could be vanquished by eliminating the Jews with the aid of the concrete forms of *Zivilisation* itself (industry, the organization of labor, the "production" system). The incarnation of capitalism was to be destroyed by industrial methods (a factory that produced death).[56] The Jew, a fetishized social figure and a biological metaphor for the modern world, was the catalyst for regenerative reaction: through the destruction of the Jew, technology could be regenerated and placed at the service of nature. The religion of nature—or, if you prefer, National Socialist biopolitics—was thus represented as a form of reactionary modernism capable of realizing a synthesis between counter-Enlightenment feeling and scientism, between obscurantism and technology, between an archaic mythology and a totalitarian order, between medieval persecutions and racial biology, and between pogroms against the Jews and their cold, impersonal, and mechanical elimination, as in an abattoir.

Regenerative anti-Semitism—which finally, within the framework of World War II, led to a vast operation of genocide—is the clue to the historical uniqueness of National Socialism. It was a product of German history (along with the latter's specific modalities of acceding to modernity and national unity), and it was the pillar the Nazi vision of the world rested on. Many historical factors contributed to the radicalization of German anti-Semitism and transformed it into the ideology of the political movement that managed to appropriate power: the persistence, up until 1918 at least, of political structures of the Ancien Regime; the tensions created by a process of industrialization and intense, rapid, and destructive social modernization in the last quarter of the nineteenth century; the social and political crisis engendered by the defeat and collapse of Kaiser Wilhelm's Reich; the intrinsic fragility of the republican institutions that replaced the latter; and the geopolitical position of Germany, which as early as 1918 placed it at the center of the clash between revolution and counterrevolution on a continental scale (a "European civil war"). But it would be a mistake to deduce from all this that those historical circumstances had isolated Germany from the West and had set it on a separate "special path."[57] On the contrary, these circumstances made it the laboratory of the West, one that synthesized a collection of elements—nationalism, racism, anti-Semitism, imperialism, anti-Bolshevism, antihumanism, and counter-Enlightenment feeling—all of which existed throughout Europe but which elsewhere either remained muted or else never entered into toxic combination.

# CONCLUSION

This genealogical study sets the Nazi violence within the long-term context of European history, but does not suggest that it stemmed from the latter automatically, ineluctably, in accordance with a pitiless and fatal causality. Even if Auschwitz was a product of Western civilization, it would be overly simplistic to see it as the natural outcome of that civilization—rather, it might be interpreted as a *pathological* manifestation of it. What we need to do is seize upon the concatenation of elements that made the Nazi extermination possible. The crime took place and it now illuminates the mental landscape in which it happened, providing us with precious evidence to use like investigating detectives to identify the victims, the murderer, and his accomplices, the motivations for the crime and the means used to perpetrate it.[1] In this work, the paradigm of a detective investigation has been applied to the analysis of the blindingly visible "clues" left by Nazism.[2] The work of identifying the victims (first and foremost the Jews, then the Gypsies, the Slavs, the anti-Fascists), the assassin (Nazi Germany), and the murderer's accomplices (Europe) was laborious but has long been completed. But what is more controversial is the definition of the motives (racism, anti-Semitism, eugenics, anti-Communism) and the weapons used in the crime (warfare, conquest, industrial extermination). Nazism certainly reinterpreted those motives and weapons in a new way, but they were all part of the context of Western civilization, in the widest sense of the expression. Some of the clues to be found in the Hitlerian discourse, such as racial biology, have been the subject of an in-depth historiographical analysis. Others that have more to do with "mental attitudes"[3] have not as yet received enough attention. The idea that civilization implies the conquest and extermination of "inferior" or "harmful" races, and the instrumental concept of technology as a means for the organized elimination of the enemy were not invented by the Nazis but had been notions familiar in Europe ever since the nineteenth century and the advent of industrial society. The genealogy traced in the present study emphasizes the fact that the violence and crimes of Nazism emerged from certain common bases of Western culture. It does not show that Auschwitz revealed the fundamental essence of the West; however, it does suggest that it was one of its possible products and, in that sense, was one if its legitimate offspring.

The uniqueness of Nazism thus lies not in its *opposition* to the West, but in its capacity to find a way to *synthesize* the West's various forms of violence. World War II was when all the elements identified in this genealogical study came together. The war was conceived as a clash between different ideologies, civilizations, "races," in short as a *Weltanschauungskrieg.* Obsessive eugenics, racist impulses, geopolitical aims, and ideological crusading converged in a single wave of destruction. The Jews—regarded as the incarnation of *Zivilisation,* the ruling group in the USSR, the inspirers of Marxism, the living antithesis of the idea of *Lebensraum,* the bacillus that was destroying the Aryan race, and the brains behind the international Communist movement—found themselves at the heart of a titanic war of conquest and annihilation and thus became the catalyst for Nazi violence. The guillotine, the abattoir, the Fordist factory, and rational administration, along with racism, eugenics, the massacres of the colonial wars and those of World War I had already fashioned the social universe and the mental landscape in which the Final Solution would be conceived and set in motion. All those elements combined to create the technological, ideological, and cultural premises for that Final Solution, by constructing an anthropological context in which Auschwitz became a possibility. These elements lay at the heart of Western civilization and had been deployed in the Europe of industrial capitalism, in the age of classic liberalism.

Until 1941, Hitler probably had no definite plan for methodically exterminating the Jews; the Final Solution was the product of the ceaseless interaction between his radical anti-Semitism and the circumstances of the war. It was this interaction that engendered the stages, forms, and means of the deportation and slaughter of the Jews. But even though it lacked a central plan, National Socialism was provided with many models, which it did not hesitate to follow. Some were ideological (racism, eugenics), political (Italian Fascism), or historical (imperialism and colonialism); others were technological and social (the rationalization of forms of domination, total warfare, serialized extermination, etc.)—but all had their origins in the context of the European civilization. From this point of view, the singularity of the genocide of the Jews seems to be less an event "without precedent"—an event without comparable historical example with regard either to "its dimensions" or to "its total configuration," in Raul Hilberg's words[4]—than a *unique synthesis* of a vast range of modes of domination and extermination already tried out separately in the course of modern Western history.[5] It was the synthesis that was unique and therefore radically and terribly new, to the point of being unimaginable and incomprehensible to many of its contemporaries. As we look back, we can see that the fusion of historical experiences and models of reference, some openly acknowledged, some subconscious or even unconscious, points to the historical genealogy of National Socialism. It would be fair to say that if ever there was a German *Sonderweg,* it may be detected not in the Prussian Empire and the process of national unification but under the Nazi regime from 1933 onward. It led not to the origins but to the ultimate destination of Nazism.[6]

Hilberg's somewhat trenchant declaration thus prompts an observation that can be formulated borrowing the words of the historian Marc Bloch, the cofounder of the *Annales d'histoire économique et sociale.* He recognized European feudalism to be a social structure that "certainly bore the imprint of a particular time and a particular place" but at the same time, by "cutting across comparative history," was able to show that many of its features were shared by traditional Japan. He concluded that feudalism was not "an event that happened in the world only once."[7] In the wake of Bloch, it could similarly be said that even if the Final Solution "certainly bore the imprint of a particular time and place," some of its features had already characterized the wars of conquest, other campaigns of extermination, and other waves of counterrevolutionary reaction. At the risk of being repetitive, let me stress that the present genealogy should not be understood teleologically. Roger Chartier has remarked of the French Revolution that although it certainly did have intellectual, cultural, and other origins, "its own history is not encompassed by them."[8] Those words apply equally well to Nazism. Even if industrial extermination does presuppose a factory and a rational administration, that is not to say that it stems ineluctably from them, nor that any capitalist enterprise is bound to constitute a potential death camp, nor that there is a dormant Eichmann inside every official. The Final Solution exploited the results of scientific research, in particular chemical research, and made use of numerous doctors, anthropologists, and eugenicists, and this certainly reveals the destructive potential of science; however, it does not reduce medicine to a science of death. The colonial massacres introduced practices of extermination that were later to be applied and exceeded by Nazism; but that does not establish a relationship of cause and effect between the two. All the same, that observation is not particularly reassuring. There are no grounds for ruling out the possibility that in the future, other syntheses equally if not more destructive might again crystallize. The atomic bombs dropped on Hiroshima and Nagasaki show that anti-Enlightenment feeling is not a necessary premise for techno-logical massacres. Both the atomic bomb and the Nazi camps were part of the "civilizing process," and within it they consti-tuted an expression of one of its potentialities, one of its faces, one of its possible offshoots, not a countertendency or an aber-ration, as Norbert Elias believes (he regards the genocide of the Jews to be "a throwback to the barbarism and savagery of ear-lier ages").[9] On the other hand, neither does the absence of causality here mean that everything can be reduced to fortu-itous and purely formal affinities. The architects of the Nazi camps were well aware that they were building factories of death, and Hitler made no secret of the fact that the conquest of *Lebensraum* followed the precedent set by the colonial wars of the nineteenth century (indeed, as he saw it, they in fact legit-imated it). The massacres of the imperialist conquests and the Final Solution are linked by more than "phenomenological affinities"[10] and distant analogies.[11] Between them runs a his-torical continuity that makes liberal Europe the laboratory of the violences of the twentieth century, and Auschwitz an au-thentic product of Western civilization.[12]

# NOTES

## Introduction

1. Diner 2000 a, p. 165.
2. Arendt 1977, p. 279.
3. S. Friedländer 1993, pp. 82–83; Traverso 1999, pp. 128–40.
4. Habermas 1978b, p. 163.
5. Mayer 1990, p. 8; see also Traverso 1992, p. 146.
6. Braudel, p. 12.
7. Vidal-Naquet, p. 256.
8. Tocqueville 1967, p. 81.
9. Chartier 1990, p. 17.
10. Hobsbawm 1999.
11. Broszat, pp. 129–73. See also S. Friedländer 1993, p. 91–92. These theses have been the subject of a rich correspondence between Broszat and Friedländer (Broszat and Friedländer 1990).
12. Mommsen, p. 399.
13. Diner 1987, p. 73.
14. Nolte 2000.
15. Furet 1999; Furet and Nolte 1998.
16. Goldhagen.
17. Nolte 2000, pp. 27, 582, 594.
18. Nolte 1987, p. 45.
19. Nolte 2000, pp. 557–558.
20. Ibid., p. 541.
21. Nolte 1987, p. 45.
22. Hamann; Kershaw 1999, p. 239.
23. Mayer 1971, p. 33. On Fascism as a "revolution against revolution," see Neocleous 1997. The "revolutionary" nature of Fascism is underlined by Sternhell 1997, and Mosse 1999.

24. Furet, p. 24. For a critique of this thesis of Furet's, see Berger and Maler 1996, pp. 17–57, and Bensaïd, p. 166.
25. Furet, p. 2.
26. Hayes, p. 101.
27. Borkenau, p. 17.
28. Croce, vol. 2, pp. 46–50; see also Bobbio, pp. 166–77.
29. See the remarks of Rousso 2001, p. 691.
30. Goldhagen, p. 11.
31. Ibid., p. 8.
32. Ibid., p. 167.
33. Ibid., p. 14.
34. Wistrich, pp. 152–60.
35. Goldhagen, p. 594, n. 53.
36. Habermas 1987a, p. 75; see also the *Laudatio* of Goldhagen produced by Habermas (1997), pp. 13–14. On Goldhagen and Habermas, see Traverso 1997b, pp. 17–26. For an excellent perspective on this whole debate, see Finchelstein 1999a.
37. Mayer 1981.
38. C. Maier 1997, pp. 29–56; Salvati, chapters 1 and 2.
39. Bloch 1974, p. 41.
40. Arendt 1994, pp. 328–60. For clarification on the concept of a "genealogy" and its use in history, beyond Nietzsche and Foucault, see Chartier 1998a, pp. 132–60.
41. Arendt 1976.
42. Said 1978; Said 1993.
43. Sternhell 1989; Sternhell 1997.
44. Mosse 1964; Mosse 1978.
45. On this subject, see the debate in Lal and Bartov 1998, pp. 1187–94.

# 1. Discipline, Punishing, Killing

1. Cited in Arasse, pp. 65–66.
2. De Maistre, vol. 4, p. 33.
3. Berlin 1992, pp. 100–74.
4. Caillois 1964, p. 33; Bée, pp. 843–62; de Becque, p. 114.
5. Kantorowicz.
6. Walzer.
7. Corbin, pp. 127–29.
8. Sofsky 1998, p. 112.
9. Brossat 1998, p. 124.
10. Arasse, p. 11.
11. In the nineteenth century, this was still the opinion of Edgar Quinet and Michelet; see Mayer 2000, p. 106. The extraordinary impact of the guillotine on nineteenth-century culture has been analyzed in particular by Gerould.
12. Arasse, p. 151. We should remember that, in a letter to Konrad Engelbert Oelsner written in 1795, the German anatomist Samuel Thomas Soemmering

challenged the dominant view that the guillotine was a vector of "humaniza-
tion" (Weidemann).
13. Cited in Arasse, p. 162.
14. Kafka, pp. 197–234; Traverso 1997a, pp. 50–57.
15. Anders 1981, p. 189.
16. Foucault p. 155. In the wake of Foucault, see above all Ignatieff and Perrot.
For an approach more influenced by Norbert Elias, cf. Spierenburg. An assess-
ment of this historiographical debate can be found in Garland, and this is
brought up to date in Brossat 2001.
17. Marx and Engels, p. 43.
18. Marx, p. 427.
19. Weber 1956, vol. 2, p. 873.
20. On Bentham's *Panopticon,* see Melossi and Pavarini, pp. 67–69, and Perrot, pp.
65–100.
21. This metamorphosis is at the center of the classic study by Louis Chevalier.
22. For an analysis of the English case, see Ignatieff.
23. Venturi, p. 140. On the debate among English reformers, see also Ignatieff.
24. Ruche and Kirchheimer (pp. 218–54) analyze in particular the English, German, and American cases; on France, see O'Brian 1982, pp. 150–90.
25. Ruche and Kirchheimer, p. 253.
26. Doray, p. 69.
27. De Gaudemar, pp. 16–23.
28. Ruche and Kirchheimer, p. 252.
29. Ibid., p. 248–49.
30. Perrot, p. 200.
31. Levi, pp. 96–97.
32. Ibid., p. 83.
33. Marx, pp. 774–86. On the basis of this critique of the system of the workhouses,
certain writers have detected in Marx an *ante litteram* critique of totalitarianism; see Losurdo 1991, pp. 75–76.
34. Sofsky 1995, p. 214. Sofsky makes this remark in connection with slavery, after
showing the differences that separate slavery, and likewise prisons, from the
Nazi concentration camps.
35. Neumann.
36. Herbert and Templer.
37. Peukert, p. 128.
38. Sellier, p. 103.
39. Corbin, pp. 137–39.
40. Vialles, pp. 21–23.
41. Sinclair, p. 377. See the commentaries by Pick 1993, pp. 182–85.
42. Kracauer 1960, p. 305.
43. S. Friedländer 1997, p. 471.
44. Cited in Hilberg, p. 837.
45. Lanzmann, p. 83. "The history of the organization of the holocaust," Z. Bauman wrote (p. 150), "could be contained in a handbook of scientific management."
46. Müller.

47. Ibid., pp. 43, 45.
48. Pressac.
49. Anders 1980, p. 22.
50. Taylor. For a presentation of Taylor's ideas, see Bravermann.
51. Taylor, p. 59; see also Pouget (1998), p. 97.
52. Céline 1952, p. 225.
53. Gramsci, vol. 3, p. 2165.
54. Levi 1988, p. 37.
55. Ford.
56. Améry, p. 44.
57. Jünger 1980a. "Militiaman of work," as suggested by Delio Cantimori, seems to me to catch the spirit of Jünger's text better than the literal translation "worker." See Cantimori; see also Michaud, p. 312–13.
58. Rabinbach 1978, pp. 137–71.
59. The autobiography of Henry Ford had been published in the "National-Socialist Library" and Hitler had expressed his admiration for the American industrialist in his conversations with Martin Bormann (Hitler 1952, vol. 1, p. 271). Ford's chief admirer was the Nazi engineer Schwerber (1930); on this subject, see Herf, chapter 8.
60. On the critique of Taylorism by DINTA, see Rabinbach 1992, pp. 284–88.
61. Weber 1978, vol. 2, p. 975.
62. Hilberg, p. 288. This passage contains an allusion to the speech Himmler addressed to the SS chiefs in October 1943. Nowadays it is possible to listen to a recording of it in the Karlhorst Museum, Berlin.
63. Browning, pp. 125–44.
64. Aly and Roth, p. 19.
65. Neumann (1987).
66. Hilberg, p. 55.
67. Elias (1973–75).
68. Adorno, p. 85.

## 2. Conquest

1. On the myth of the "dark continent" see Brantlinger 1998, pp. 173–97.
2. Conrad, pp. 152–53.
3. Arendt 1976, pp. 171–75.
4. Schmitt 1974, p. 190.
5. Mill, pp. 14–15; Parekh, pp. 81–98. On the colonialist background to theories of international law, see Tuck.
6. Cited in Said 1994, p. 108.
7. Tocqueville 1961, vol. 1, p. 67.
8. W. Cohen, pp. 377–78.
9. Tocqueville 1991, vol. 1, pp. 704, 698. See Le Cour Grandmaison and Edward Said, who in this connection speaks of genocide in Algeria (Said 1993, pp. 218–21).
10. Said 1993; Adas, pp. 199–210.

11. Rivet, p. 127–38.
12. Jünger 1980a, pp. 329–30.
13. Korsch, p. 3; Jones, p. 203.
14. Arendt 1976, p. 221.
15. Brantlinger 1988, pp. 24–25; Davis, pp. 32–33.
16. Ratzel. On the history of the idea of Lebensraum, see Lange; Smith; and Kershaw 1999, pp. 364–69.
17. Wippermann, pp. 85–104.
18. Korinman, pp. 34, 58, 62.
19. Wehler, p. 212. The elements of continuity between the imperialist goals of the Prussian Empire during World War I and the Nazi plans for the conquest of the "living space" have been generally recognized by German historiography since the "Fischer controversy" of 1961; see Husson, chapter 3.
20. Cited in Warmbold, p. 191.
21. Cited in Brantlinger 1988, p. 23.
22. Lukàcs, p. 537. The chapter on social Darwinism remains valuable even in a work whose general theses nowadays seem dated. On the formation of Social Darwinism, see Claeys.
23. Lee, p. xcviii. See Burrow, pp. 137–54, and Rainger, pp. 51–70. On the perception of Africa in nineteenth-century English culture, cf. Lorimer. This debate is also mentioned by Lindqvist, p. 173.
24. Ibid., p. xcix.
25. Bendyshe, p. c.
26. Ibid., p. cvi.
27. Wallace 1864, pp. clxiv–clxv.
28. Ibid., pp. clxv, 53–54.
29. Wallace 1891, p. 185; Van Oosterzee; Pichot, pp. 94–97.
30. Kidd, pp. 48–49. On Kidd, who apparently modified his imperialism and even criticized eugenics toward the end of his life, see Crook.
31. Cited in Bernardini, p. 145.
32. Bonwick.
33. Panoff, p. 439, citing Marestang.
34. Ibid., p. 445, citing Caillot, pp. 77–78.
35. On the reception of this book by Darwin from an imperialist point of view, from the moment it appeared, see De Roy, pp. 10–11.
36. Pichot, p. 99; Gay, pp. 45–53.
37. Cited in La Vergata, p. 327, and Darwin, "Notebook E," pp. 63–64.
38. Cited in La Vergata, p. 326, and Darwin 1839, p. 520.
39. Darwin 1981, vol. 1, p. 210. This thesis was criticized by Bonwick, p. 380.
40. Darwin 1981, chapter 7.
41. Gumplowicz, p. 247.
42. Turner, p. 3.
43. Cited in Stannard, p. 172.
44. Cited in Hofstadter, p. 174.
45. Cited in Bequemont, p. 157.
46. Cited in Hofstadter, p. 175.
47. Grant, pp. 50–51.

48. W. Cohen, pp. 292–362.
49. Reade, p. 583.
50. Ibid., p. 586.
51. Ibid., p. 587.
52. On this subject see the fundamental study by Brantlinger 1995, pp. 43–56.
53. Grenville, p. 165.
54. Blackbourn, p. 426; Arendt 1976, p. 185. On the atrocities perpetrated by German troops at the time of the repression of the Boxers, see P. Cohen, pp. 184–85.
55. Wesseling, pp. 3–4.
56. Etamad, p. 113.
57. Ellis, p. 18; Killingray, p. 147.
58. Cited in Landes, p. 553.
59. Howard, p. 132; Parker, p. 136.
60. Cited in Maspero, p. 175; Etamad, p. 131.
61. Ageron, pp. 12–14.
62. Hochschild, pp. 264–65; Gay, pp. 87–88; Etamad, p. 132.
63. Etamad, pp. 129–135.
64. Ibid., pp. 134–35, 291–301. On the use of the famine in India as an instrument of colonial domination, see Davis.
65. Helbig, pp. 102–11.
66. Bridgman, pp. 127–29. General von Trotha's order to proceed to the extermination is reproduced in Dreschler, p. 138. On the historiographical debate on the genocide of the Hereros, see Krüger, pp. 62–68.
67. Bridgman, pp. 131, 164.
68. Krüger, pp. 65–66.
69. Walser Smith, pp. 107–24.
70. Hake 1998, p. 179.
71. Cited in Del Boca 1995, pp. 334.
72. Del Boca 1996, p. 75, citing telegram of June 8, 1936.
73. Del Boca 1995, pp. 336–37.
74. De Felice, pp. 236–39.
75. Rochat; Tranfaglia, p. 670; Milza, pp. 672–73, Labanca, pp. 145–63.
76. Burleigh 1988.
77. Madajzyk, pp. 12–17; Graml 1993, p. 450.
78. Cited in Aly, p. 285.
79. On the syncretism of the Nazi vision of the world, see Mayer 1988, p. 114.
80. Schmitt 1991, p. 68.
81. Ibid., p. 69.
82. Picker, pp. 464–465. In his private conversations, Hitler made no secret of his bitterness in the face of the Japanese expansion in Asia, for despite the German alliance with imperial Japan, it inevitably implied "a retreat of the white man"—Great Britain. See Kershaw 2000, p. 730. On Rosenberg's admiration of Great Britain, see Cecil, p. 162.
83. Field, p. 355.
84. Hitler 1952, vol. 1, p. 25. The relation between the colonial tradition and total war is underlined in Losurdo 1996, pp. 179–255.

85. Ibid., p. 34.
86. Ibid., p. 16.
87. Ibid., p. 68.
88. Ibid., p. 69.
89. Hitler 1952, vol. 2, p. 252. It is perhaps worth recording, as trivial history, that Hitler had always been a fan of Karl May, an extremely popular German writer of stories about cowboys and Indians (Burleigh 2000, p. 93).
90. Hitler 1952, p. 286. On Hitler's ideas on the subject of the conquered territories, see Bullock, vol. 2, pp. 188–201.
91. Picker, p. 119.
92. Nolte 2000, p. 545. Apparently Koch was in the habit of calling the Ukrainians "white Negroes" (Cecil 1972, p. 198).
93. Bartov 1999, p. 187.
94. Ibid., p. 183.
95. Ibid., p. 195.
96. Hillgruber 1986, pp. 24–25. On Hillgruber, see Anderson, pp. 54–65.
97. Habermas 1987a, pp. 63–67.
98. Nolte 1987, p. 45.
99. Graml, p. 440–51.
100. Cited in Reuth, p. 331. In this respect, Nazism inherited the typically German opposition drawn between *Zivilisation,* the whole body of material and technical conquests of an age, and *Kultur,* the spiritual patrimony of a nation and, more generally, Europe. On the cleavage between this and the French (and British) notion of *civilization,* which does not recognize such a dichotomy, and the German notion of *Zivilisation,* see Curtius.
101. Cited in Reuth, p. 482.
102. Cecil, p. 199.
103. Cited in Reuth, p. 482.
104. S. Friedländer 1997, chapter 3, pp. 73–112.
105. Hitler 1943, p. 752. On this aspect, see above all Diner 1999, p. 220.

## 3. Destruction: Total War

1. Gibelli, pp. 91–95.
2. Keegan, p. 234.
3. Cited in Leed, chapter 3.
4. C. Maier, pp. 95–134.
5. Rabinbach, pp. 259–70.
6. Winter.
7. Keegan, pp. 245–47; Kern, chapter 11.
8. Weber 1988, p. 321.
9. Ibid., p. 322.
10. Cited in Keegan, p. 318.
11. Ellis, p. 55.
12. Ibid., p. 91.
13. Diner 1999, pp. 44–45.

14. Howard, p. 123.
15. H. Maier, pp. 16–18.
16. Cited in Leed, chapter 3.
17. Becker, p. 50.
18. Jünger 1980b, p. 114.
19. Hüppauf 1997, p. 19.
20. Gibelli, pp. 108–9.
21. Caillois 1951, p. 106.
22. Ibid., p. 107.
23. Cited in Dagen, p. 104.
24. Norton Cru, p. 127.
25. Leed, chapter 3.
26. Bartov 2000, p. 111.
27. Keegan, pp. 261, 285.
28. Jünger.
29. Revelli.
30. Fussel, chapter 2.
31. Bartov 2000, pp. 12–14.
32. Bloch 1992, pp. 104–26.
33. Browning 1994.
34. Eksteins, p. 157; Audoin-Rouzeau and Becker, p. 76.
35. Becker, pp. 230–33.
36. Ibid., p. 236.
37. Arendt 1976, pp. 275–90. Not having seen the phenomenon of civilian internees and deportees during World War I, Arendt tended to consider "stateless people" as a product of the treaties of 1919.
38. Procacci, pp. 168–70.
39. Cited in Procacci, p. 279.
40. Audoin-Rouzeau and Becker, pp. 85–105; Wieviorka.
41. Norton Cru, p. 32; Bartov 1996a, p. 33.
42. Levi 1988, p. 2.
43. Cited in Dagen, p. 240.
44. Fussel, chapter 5.
45. Cited in Procacci, p. 113.
46. Procacci, p. 118.
47. Fussel, chapter 5.
48. Levi, p. 6.
49. Simpson; p. 172, Fussel chapter 5.
50. Benjamin 1977a, p. 386.
51. Dagen, p. 313.
52. Audoin-Rouzeau and Becker, p. 40.
53. Reemtsma, pp. 377–401.
54. Bartov 1996a, p. 23.
55. Hobsbawm 1997, pp. 253–65.
56. Mosse 1990, p. 160.
57. Anders 1983, p. 221.
58. Becker 1998, p. 328.

59. Ibid., pp. 323, 330; Horne, pp. 133–46; and Hans-Jürgen Lüsebrink, pp. 57–85.
60. Mosse 1990, pp. 159–81.
61. Hüppauf 1993, pp. 43–84.
62. Theweleit, vol. 2, pp. 228–38.
63. Jünger 1997.
64. Schmitt 1996, p. 27; Kohn, p. 64.
65. Wismann, pp. 56–57.
66. Mosse 1974.
67. Krumeich, p. 40.
68. Papini, p. 208; cited in Isnenghi, p. 94.
69. Neocleous, chapters 2 and 3.
70. Cited in Benjamin 1977b, p. 168.
71. Jünger 1997, p. 71.
72. Ibid., p. 95. Some writers, generalizing unjustifiably, have considered this literature to reflect an essential feature of warfare as a masculine experience, which goes way beyond the Fascist interpretation; see Bourke.
73. Benjamin 1973a, vol. 3, p. 249.
74. Benjamin 1978, pp. 241–42.
75. Benjamin 1973b, vol. 4, 1, p. 476; Löwy 1993, pp. 175–84; Leslie, chapter 1.

## 4. Classification and Repression

1. Cited in Heer, p. 116. For a well-documented analysis of the central notion of "Jewish Bolshevism" in German military propaganda during the 1941–43 period, see Übershär and Wette (1984), and above all Streit.
2. Cited in Jahn, p. 49.
3. Cited in Kershaw 2000, p. 685.
4. Kenz; p. 304, Mayer 2000, pp. 515–26.
5. Siva 1920; Miccoli, pp. 1550–51.
6. Cited in Schor, p. 29.
7. Cohn; Taguieff 1992.
8. Webster, p. 293; Friedländer 1997, pp. 99–100.
9. Poliakov, vol. 2, pp. 420–30.
10. Cited in Nolte 2000, pp. 138–39.
11. Cited in Bédaria, pp. 177–78. The anti-Semitic poster is reproduced in King, p. 56.
12. Mann, p. 223; see also Darmann, p. 128.
13. Diner 1999, pp. 48–53; Burleigh 2000, p. 38. On Rosenberg's upbringing see Cecil.
14. Nolte 2000.
15. Cited in Kershaw 1998, p. 360.
16. Jäckel, p. 79.
17. Rosenberg 1986, p. 189; Rosenberg 1922; Nolte 2000, pp. 143–44. Rosenberg's brochure was reprinted several times by the Nazi party's publisher, Franz Eher of Munich. A more "theoretical" and less propagandist concept of this view of Bolshevism as a Jewish creation was developed by Leibbrandt.

18. Hitler 1943, p. 772; Kershaw 1998, p. 361.
19. Sontag.
20. Proctor 1999.
21. Ibid., chapter 2.
22. For a reconstruction of this cultural context see Nye 1975; Barrows; Mucchielli.
23. Evans 1992, pp. 149–73. For an analysis of two concrete historical experiences see Delaporte 1990 and Evans 1987.
24. Nye 1984. Alain Brossat uses the word "zoopolitical" to describe the "demoniacal" pact sealed at the time between bioscience, positivist ideology, and social Darwinism (Brossat 1998, p. 137).
25. Delaporte 1995, p. 54; Chevalier, p. 711.
26. Burke, p. 164; Toqueville 1986, p. 767.
27. Balibar, pp. 272–88; Burgio, pp. 9–26.
28. Kuklick, p. 100.
29. Ibid., p. 103.
30. Le Bon 1919, p. 41, Taguieff 1998, pp. 73–81; Sternhell 1997, pp. 182–90.
31. Le Bon 1919, p. 65.
32. Vacher de la Pouge 1909, pp. 227–71; Taguieff 1998, p. 112; Sternhell 1997, pp. 204–12.
33. Tombs, p. 345.
34. Ibid., p. 346.
35. Ruffié and Sournia, pp. 278–80.
36. Lidsky, p. 49.
37. Ibid., p. 46.
38. Zola, p. 476.
39. Ibid., p. 508.
40. Taine, p. 168.
41. Ibid., p. 192.
42. Ibid., p. 191.
43. Ibid., p. 192.
44. Ibid., p. 191.
45. Ibid., p. 123.
46. Cited in Lidsky, pp. 60–65.
47. Tarde (1892); p. 358; Barrows, p. 128.
48. Pick 1989, chapter 3.
49. Blankaert, pp. 60–61.
50. Bordier, p. 297; Blankaert, p. 62.
51. Lombroso.
52. Cited in Darmon, p. 57.
53. Lombroso and Lachi, p. 35. On this subject, see Villa. Among the French students of Lombroso who devoted themselves to this theme, see Hamon and Proal. On the French debates about the theory of the "born criminal" see Nye 1984, pp. 97–131 and Mucchielli, pp. 58–79.
54. Sighele, pp. 86–89.
55. Le Bon 1995, pp. 94, 100; Le Bon 1912, pp. 651–53.
56. Sternhell 1997, pp. xxxvi–xl.

57. Mosca; Pareto.
58. Michels, pp. 295–303.
59. Ibid., p. 151.
60. Cited in Mitzman, p. 323.
61. Gilman, pp. 78–79.
62. Meige, pp. 343, 355.
63. Cited in Rabinbach 1992, p. 156.
64. Drumont, vol. 1, pp. 106–10.
65. Leroy-Beaulieu, pp. 190–91, 225.
66. Bacharach, pp. 179–90; Schulte, pp. 339–54.
67. Birnbaum 1992.
68. Bartov 1996b, p. 131.
69. Klee.
70. Hilberg, p. 757.
71. Pichot, pp. 207–13.
72. Moriani (1999), p. 58.
73. Proctor 1988, pp. 97–101; Kühl.
74. Kevles 1995, p. 89.
75. Ammon, pp. 317–18; Pichot, pp. 59–60.
76. Cited in Koch, p. 111.
77. Hart, p. 238; Pick, 1993, p. 80.
78. Marinetti; Richard, pp. 34–37.
79. Novicow; p. 3; Pichot, p. 54.
80. Pogliano 1984; Pogliano 1999.
81. Israel and Nastasi.
82. Vacher de Lapouge 1896, p. 472. On this subject see Taguieff 1998, p. 126.
83. Cited in Taguieff 1998, p. 143. On Vacher de la Pouge's contribution to the eu-
    genicist foundations of Nazism, cf. Sternhell 1985 and Hecht.
84. Carol, p. 169.
85. Ibid., p. 170.
86. Carrel, p. 235; Burrin, p. 356; Drouard.
87. Weindling, p. 257.
88. Ibid., p. 275.
89. Proctor 1988.
90. On the transition from "positive" eugenics to voluntary sterilization to the
    "negative" eugenics of the 1933 law on enforced sterilization, see Noaks, p. 86;
    S. Friedländer 1997, pp. 39–40; Pollack, pp. 80–81; Massin, pp. 197–262.
91. Bock.
92. Pollack, p. 81.
93. Kevles, p. 168; Kühl, pp. 86–87; Pichot, pp. 205–6.
94. Pick 1989, p. 238.
95. Pichot, p. 276.
96. Pick 1989, pp. 238–39.

## 5. Extermination: Nazi Anti-Semitism

1. Simmel, p. 265.
2. Ibid., p. 601.
3. Cited in Poliakov, vol. 2, p. 298.
4. Leroy-Beaulieu, p. 196.
5. Ibid., p. 193.
6. Ibid., p. 209.
7. Gide, p. 763.
8. Sartre (1954), pp. 136, 137.
9. Drumont, p. 251.
10. Winock (1982), pp. 117–44; Holz, pp. 258–358.
11. Céline 1937, pp. 183, 185.
12. Drieu la Rochelle, p. 100.
13. Spengler, p. 950.
14. Sombart 1913, pp. 271–73.
15. Sombart 1920, p. 242.
16. Ibid., pp. 320–21, 327.
17. Cited in Lenger, p. 199.
18. Sternhell 1989, p. 32.
19. Steyn, pp. 42–56 and 31–41.
20. Ford, pp. 22–24.
21. Herf.
22. Jünger 1989.
23. Jünger 1930; Evard, pp. 113–14.
24. Haushofer 1986, pp. 185–91.
25. Cited in Diner 2000b, pp. 26–48.
26. Cited in Jacobsen, p. 31.
27. Schmitt 1933, p. 1; Gross (2000), p. 68.
28. Schmitt 1993, pp. 9–10.
29. Ibid., p. 15.
30. Ibid., p. 25.
31. Schmitt 1936, p. 28; Gross, p. 129.
32. Schmitt 1982, pp. 106–8.
33. Schmitt 1988a, pp. 235–39.
34. Schmitt 1988b, p. 295.
35. Schmitt 1991, p. 79; Ratzel, p. 67.
36. Ibid., p. 79.
37. Ibid., p. 79; Ratzel, p. 12.
38. Schmitt (1991), p. 81.
39. Wismann, p. 48.
40. Cited in Beyerchen, pp. 88–89.
41. Stark and Müller; Beyerchen, pp. 132–33; Israel and Nastasi, pp. 310–11.
42. Traverso 1997c.
43. Kershaw 1998, p. 362; S. Friedländer 1997, p. 178–80; Burleigh 2000, pp. 90–94.
44. Goebbels 1971, p. 108.

45. Diner 2000c, pp. 49–77.
46. Dupeux, pp. 201–21; Sternhell 1989, p. 20.
47. Hitler 1952, vol. 1, p. 321.
48. Pois.
49. Siebert (1941), Pois (1993), p. 175.
50. S. Friedländer 1997, p. 87.
51. Kohn, p. 69.
52. Agamben, p. 164–65.
53. Kershaw 2000, p. 252.
54. Aron, p. 926.
55. Mayer 1990, pp. 114–35.
56. Postone, pp. 242–54.
57. Kershaw 1998, pp. 132–33. For a systematic critique of the *Sonderweg,* see Blackbourn and Eley. The whole debate is very well summarized in Finchelstein 1999b.

## Conclusion

1. This was the method that Kracauer adopted, despite its inevitably schematic nature in the early postwar years.
2. Ginzburg, pp. 158–209.
3. Chartier 1998b, pp. 34, 36, 44.
4. Hilberg, p. 8.
5. Bauman, p. xiii.
6. Steinmetz, p. 257.
7. Bloch 1994, pp. 610–12.
8. Chartier 1990, p. 21.
9. Elias 1996, p. 302. On this debate, see Chartier 1991, p. 28; Traverso 1997a, pp. 231–34; Löwy 2001, pp. 9–19.
10. Such as those seized upon by Yerushalmi between the statutes on "blood purity" of the Spanish Inquisition and the Nuremberg Laws: See Yerushalmi 1998, p. 259.
11. Such as those indicated by Arno J. Mayer (1990, p. 38) between the genocide of the Jews and the total war of the twentieth century on the one hand, and the Thirty Years War or the First Crusade on the other. Cf. Mayer (1990), p. 38.
12. Ernest Mandel (1986, p. 91) thus identified the seed of the Jewish genocide in colonialist and imperialist racism.

# BIBLIOGRAPHY

Adas, Michael. 1989. *Machines as the Measure of Men: Science, Technology, and Ideologies of Western Dominance*. Ithaca and London: Cornell University Press.

Adorno, Theodor W. 1969. "Erziehung nach Auschwitz." In *Stichworte, kritische Modelle 2*, Frankfurt: Suhrkamp. French translation, "Eduquer après Auschwitz," *Modèles critiques* (Paris: Payot, 1979).

Agamben, Giorgio. 1995. *Homo sacer: Il potere sovrano e la nuda vita*. Torino: Einaudi. French translation, *Homo sacer* (Paris: Seuil, 1997).

Ageron, Charles Robert. 1979. *Histoire de l'Algérie contemporaine*. Vol. 2, 1871–1945. Paris: Presses Universitaires de France.

Aly, Götz. 1995. *"Endlösung": Völkerschiebung und der Mord an deneuropäischen Juden*. Frankfurt: Fischer.

Aly, Götz, and Karl-Heinz Roth. 2000. *Die restlose Erfassung: Volkszählen, Identifizieren, Aussondern im Nationalsozialismus*. Frankfurt: Fischer.

Améry, Jean. 1977. *Jenseits von Schuld und Sühne: Bewältigungsversuche eines Uberwältigten*. Stuttgart: Klett-Cotta. French translation, *Par-delà le crime et le châtiment: Essai pour surmonter l'insurmontable*. Paris: Actes Sud, 1995.

Ammon, Otto. 1900. *L'Ordre sociale et ses bases naturelles: Esquisse d'une anthroposociologie*. Paris: Albert Fontemoing.

Anders, Günther. 1980. *Die Antiquiertheit des Menschen*. 2 vols. Munich: C. H. Beck.

———. 1981. *Die atomare Drohung: Radikale Überlegungen*. Munich: C. H. Beck.

———. 1983. "Georg Grosz." In *Mensch ohne Welt: Schriften zur Kunst und Literatur*. Munich: C. H. Beck.

Anderson, Perry. 1992. "On Emplotment: Two Kinds of Ruins." In Saul Friedländer, ed., *Probing the Limits of Representation: Nazism and the "Final Solution."* Cambridge, Mass.: Harvard University Press. Reprinted in Perry Anderson, *A Zone of Engagement* (London: Verso, 1993).

Arasse, Daniel. 1987. *La Guillotine et l'imaginaire de la terreur*. Paris: Flammarion.

Arendt, Hannah. 1976. *The Origins of Totalitarianism*. New York: Harcourt, Brace.

———. 1977. *Eichmann in Jerusalem: A Report on the Banality of Evil*. New York: Penguin Books.

Aron, Raymond. 1990. "L'Avenir des réligions séculières." In *Chroniques de guerre: La France libre 1940–1945*. Paris: Gallimard.

Audoin-Rouzeau, Stéphane, and Annette Becker. 2000. *14–18: Retrouver la guerre*. Paris: Gallimard. English translation, *14–18: Understanding the Great War* (New York: Hill & Wang, 2002).

Bacharach, Walter Zwi. 1984. "Ignaz Zollschans Rassentheorie." In Walter Grab, ed., *Jüdische Indentität und Intergration in Österreich und Deutschland 1848–1918*. Tel Aviv: Jahrbuch des Instituts für Deutsche Geschichte.

Balibar, Etienne. 1988. "Le Racisme de classe." In Etienne Balibar and Immanuel Wallerstein, eds., *Race, nation, classe*. Paris: La Découverte.

Barrows, Susanna. 1990. *Miroirs déformants: Réflexions sur la foule en France à la fin du XIXe siècle*. Paris: Aubier. Translation of *Distorting Mirrors* (New Haven: Yale University Press, 1981).

Bartov, Omer. 1990. *Hitler's Army: Soldiers, Nazis and War in the Third Reich*. Oxford: Oxford University Press.

———. 1996a. "The European Imagination in the Age of Total War." In *Murder in Our Midst: The Holocaust, Industrial Killing, and Representation*. Oxford and New York: Oxford University Press.

———. 1996b. "Savage War." In Michael Burleigh, ed., *Confronting the Nazi Past: New Debates on Modern German History*. London: Collins & Brown.

———. 2000. *Mirrors of Destruction: War, Genocide, and Modern Identity*. Oxford and New York: Oxford University Press.

Bauman, Zygmunt. 1989. *Modernity and the Holocaust*. Oxford: Basil Blackwell.

Becker, Annette. 1998. *Oubliés de la Grande Guerre: Humanitaire et culture de guerre 1914–1918*. Paris: Noêsis.

Bédarida, François. 1999. *Churchill*. Paris: Fayard.

Bée, Michel. 1983. "Le Spectacle de l'exécution dans la France d'Ancien Régime." *Annales ESC*, no. 4.

Bendyshe, Thomas. 1864. "The Extinction of the Races." *Journal of the Anthropological Society*. London: Trübner & Co.

Benjamin, Walter. 1973a. "Theorien des deutschen Faschismus." *Gesammelte Schriften*. Vol. 3. Frankfurt: Suhrkamp. French translation, "Théories du fascisme allemand," *Oeuvres*, Vol. 2 (Paris: Folio-Gallimard, 2000).

———. 1973b. "Die Waffen von morgen." *Gesammelte Schriften*. Vol. 4. Frankfurt: Suhrkamp.

———. 1977a. "Der Erzähler: Betrachtungen zum Werk Nikkolai Lesskows." In *Illuminationen: Ausgewählte Schriften*. Frankfurt: Suhrkamp. French translation, "Le conteur: Réflexions sur l'oeuvre de Nicolas Leskov," *Oeuvres*, Vol. 3 (Paris: Folio-Gallimard, 2000).

———. (1977b). "Das Kunstwerk im Zeitalter seiner Reproduzierbarkeit." In *Illuminationen: Ausgewählte Schriften*. Frankfurt: Suhrkamp. French translation, "L'Oeuvre d'art à l'époque de sa reproductibilité technique," *Oeuvres*, Vol. 3. (Paris: Folio-Gallimard, 2000).

———. 1978. *Sens unique*. Paris: Les Lettres Nouvelles. Originally published as "Einbahnstrasse," *Gesammelte Schriften*, Vol. 4 (Frankfurt: Suhrkamp, 1973).

Bensaïd, Daniel. 1999. *Qui est le juge? Pour en finir avec le tribunal de l'histoire.* Paris: Fayard.

Bequemont, Daniel. 1992. "Aspects du darwinisme anglo-saxon." In P. Tort, ed., *Darwinisme et société.* Paris: Presses Universitaires de France.

Berger, Denis, and Henri Maler. 1996. *Une certaine idée du communisme: Répliques à François Furet.* Paris: Editions du Félin.

Berlin, Isaiah. 1992. "Joseph de Maistre and the Origins of Fascism." In *The Crooked Timber of Humanity: Chapters in the History of Ideas.* London: John Murray. 1990.

Bernardini, Jean-Marc. 1997. *Le Darwinisme social en France (1859–1918): Fascination et rejet d'une idéologie.* Paris: CNRS Editions.

Beyerchen, Alan. 1977. *Scientists Under Hitler: Politics and the Physics Community in the Third Reich.* New Haven and London: Yale University Press.

Birnbaum, Pierre. 1992. *Les Fous de la République: Histoire de Juifs d'état de Gambetta à Vichy.* Paris: Fayard.

Blackbourn, David. 1997. *The Long Nineteenth Century: A History of Germany 1789–1918.* Oxford: Oxford University Press.

Blackbourn, David, and Geoff Elay. 1984. *The Peculiarities of German History: Bourgeois Society and Politics in Nineteenth-Century Germany.* Oxford: Oxford University Press.

Blankaert, Claude. 1995. "Des sauvages en pays civilisé: L'Anthropologie des criminals (1850–1900)." In Laurent Mucchielli, ed., *Histoire de la criminologie française.* Paris: L'Harmatan.

Bloch, Ernst. 1992. *Erbschaft dieser Zeit.* Reprint, Frankfurt: Suhrkamp. French translation, *Héritage de ce temps* (Paris: Payot, 1978).

Bloch, Marc. 1974. *Apologie pour l'histoire.* Paris: Armand Colin.

———. 1994. *La Société féodale.* Paris: Albin Michel.

Bobbio, Norberto. 1990. *Profilo ideologico del Novecento.* Milan: Garzanti.

Bock, Gisela. 1986. *Zwangssterilisation im Nationalsozialismus: Studien zur Rassenpolitik und Frauenpolitik.* Opladen: Westdeutscher Verlag.

Bonwick, James. 1870. *The Last of the Tasmanians or the Black War of Van Diemen's Land.* London: Sampson, Low & Marston.

Bordier, Arthur. 1879. "Sur les cranes d'assassins." *Bulletin de la Société d'Anthropologie de Paris* 2.

Borkenau, Franz. 1940. *The Totalitarian Enemy.* London: Faber & Faber.

Bourke, Joanna. 1999. *An Intimate History of Killing: Face-to-Face Killing in Twentieth-Century Warfare.* London: Granta.

Brantlinger, Patrick. 1988. *Rule of Darkness: British Literature and Imperialism, 1830–1914.* Ithaca and London: Cornell University Press.

———. 1995. "Dying Races": Rationalizing Genocide in the Nineteenth Century." In Jan Nederveen Pieterse and Bhikuh Parekh, eds., *The Decolonization of Imagination: Culture, Knowledge, and Power.* London: Zed Books.

Braudel, Fernand. 1969. "Histoire et sciences socials: La Longue Duree." *Ecrits sur l'histoire.* Paris: Flammarion.

Bravermann, Harry. 1974. *Labor and Monopoly Capital: The Degradation of Work in the Twentieth Century.* New York: Monthly Review Press.

Bridgman, John M. 1981. *The Revolt of the Herero*. Berkeley, Calif.: University of California Press.

Brossat, Alain. 1998. *Le Corps de l'ennemi: hyperviolence et démocratie*. Paris: La Fabrique.

———. 2001. *Pour en finir avec la prison*. Paris: La Fabrique.

Broszat, Martin. 1987. "Plädoyer für eine Historisierung des National-Sozialismus." In *Nach Auschwitz: Der schwierige Umgang mit unserer Geschichte*. Munich: Oldenbourg. French translation, "Plaidoyer pour une historisation du national-socialisme," *Bulletin trimestriel de la Fondation Auschwitz*, no. 24 (1990).

Broszat, Martin, and Saul Friedländer. 1990. "Sur l'historisation du national-socialisme: echange de lettres." *Bulletin trimestriel de la Fondation Auschwitz*, no. 24.

Browning, Christopher. 1992. "Bureaucracy and Mass Murder: The German Administrator's Comprehension of the Final Solution." In *The Path to Genocide: Essays on Launching the Final Solution*. Cambridge, England: Cambridge University Press.

———. 1994. *Ordinary Men*. London: HarperCollins.

Bullock, Alan. 1991. *Hitler and Stalin: Parallel Lives,* London: Haynes.

Burgio, Alberto. 1998. "La razza come metafora." In *L'invenzione delle razze: Studi su razzismo e revisione storico*. Rome: Manifestolibri.

Burke, Edmund. 1986. *Reflections on the Revolution in France*. 1790. Harmondsworth: Penguin Books.

Burleigh, Michael. 1988. *Germany Turns Eastwards: A Study of Ostforschung in the Third Reich*. Cambridge, England: Cambridge University Press.

———. 2000. *The Third Reich: A New History*. London: Macmillan.

Burrin, Philippe. 1993. *La France à l'Heure Allemande: 1940–1944*. Paris: Editions du Seuil. English translation, *France Under the Germans* (New York: The New Press, 1996).

Burrow, J. W. 1963. "Evolution and Anthropology in the 1860s: The Anthropological Society of London 1863–71." *Victorian Studies*, no. 7.

Caillois, Roger. 1951. "Le Vertige de la guerre." In *Quatre essays de sociologie contemporaine*. Paris: Perrin.

———. 1964. "Sociologie du bourreau." In *Instincts et société*. Paris: Denoël/Gonthier.

Cantimori, Delio. 1991. "Note sul nazionalsocialismo." In *Politica e storia contemporanea: Scritti 1927–1942*. Turin: Einaudi.

Carol, Anne. 1995. *Histoire de l'eugénisme en France: la Médecine et la procréation, XIXe–XXe siècle*. Paris: Editions du Seuil.

Carrel, Alexis. 1956. *Jour après jour 1893–1944*. Paris: Plon.

Cecil, Robert. 1972. *The Myth of the Master Race: Alfred Rosenberg and the Nazi Ideology*. London: B. T. Batsford.

Céline, Louis-Ferdinand. 1952. *Voyage au bout de la nuit*. Paris: Folio-Gallimard.

———. 1937, *Bagatelles pour un massacre*. Paris: Denoël.

Chartier, Roger 1990. *Les Origines culturelles de la révolution française*. Paris: Seuil.

———. 1991. "Conscience de soi et lien social." Foreword to Norbert Elias, *La Société des individus*. Paris: Fayard.

————. 1998a. "La Chimère de l'origine: Michel Foucault, les Lumières et la révolution française." *Au bord de la falaise: L'Histoire entre certitude et inquiétude*. Paris: Albin Michel.

————. 1998b. "Histoire intellectuelle et histoire des mentalites." *Au bord de la falaise: L'Histoire entre certitude et inquiétude*. Paris: Albin Michel.

Chevalier, Louis. 1984. *Classes laborieuses et classes dangereuses pendant la première moitié du XIXe siècle*. Paris: Hachette.

Claeys, Gregory. 2000. "The Survival of the Fittest and the Origins of Social Darwinism." *Journal of the History of Ideas* 2, no. 62.

Cohen, Paul. 1997. *History in Three Keys: The Boxers as Event, Experience, and Myth*. New York: Columbia University Press.

Cohen, William. 1980. *Français et africains: Les Noirs dans le regard des blancs (1530–1880)*. Paris: Gallimard.

Cohn, Norman. 1967. *Histoire d'un mythe: La "Conspiration juive" et les protocols des sages de Sion*. Paris: Gallimard.

Conrad, Joseph. 1996. *Heart of Darkness/Au coeur des ténèbres*. Paris: Folio-Gallimard.

Corbin, Alain. 1990. *Le Village des cannibales*. Paris: Aubier.

Croce, Benedetto. 1963. "Chi è fascista?" 1944. In *Scritti e discorsi politici*. Bari and Rome: Laterza.

Crook, D. P. 1984. *Benjamin Kidd: Portrait of a Social Darwinist*. Cambridge, England: Cambridge University Press.

Curtius, Ernst-Robert. 1995. *Essai sur la France*. Paris: Editions de l'Aube.

Dagen, Philippe. 1996. *Le Silence des peintres: les Artistes face à la Grande Guerre*. Paris: Fayard.

Darmann, Jacques. 1995. *Thomas Mann et les juifs*. Frankfurt: Peter Lang.

Darmon, Pierre. 1989. *Médecins et assassins à la Belle Époque: La Médicalisation du crime*. Paris: Seuil.

Darwin, Charles, 1839. *Journal of Researches in Geology and Natural History*. London: Henry Colburn.

————. 1981. *La Descendance de l'homme et la selection sexuelle*. Paris: Complexe. Translation of *The Descent of Man and Selection in Relation to Sex* (London: 1871).

Davis, Mike. 2001. *Late Victorian Holocausts: El Niño, Famines and the Making of the Third World*. London: Verso.

De Becque, Antoine. 1997. *La Gloire et l'effroi: Sept morts sous la terreur*. Paris: Grasset.

De Felice, Renzo. 1993. *Storia degli ebrei italiani sotto il fascismo*. Turin: Einaudi.

Delaporte, François. 1990. *Le Savoir de la maladie: essai sur le choléra de 1832*. Paris: Presses Universitaires de France.

————. 1995. *Les Épidémies*. Paris: Cité des Sciences et de l'Industrie/Pocket.

Del Boca, Angelo. 1995. "Le leggi razziali nell'impero di Mussolini." In Angelo Del Boca, Massimo Legnani, Mario G. Rossi, eds., *Il regime fascista: storia e storiografia*. Bari and Rome: Laterza.

————. 1996. *I gas di Mussolini: il fascismo e la guerra d'Etiopia*. Rome: Editori Riuniti.

De Roy, Piet. 1990. "Ernst Haeckel's Theory of Recapitulation." In Jan Breman, ed., *Imperial Monkey Business: Racial Supremacy in Social Darwinist Theory and Colonial Practice*. Amsterdam: Vu University Press.

Diner, Dan. 1987. "Zwischen Aporie und Apologie: Über die Grenzen der Historisierbarkeit des Nationalsozialismus." In Dan Diner, ed., *Ist der Nationalsozialismus Geschichte? Zur Historisierung und Historikerstreit*. Frankfurt: Fischer.

———. 1999. *Das Jahrhundert verstehen: Eine universalhistorische Deutung*. Munich: Luchterhand.

———. 2000a. "Historical Experience and Cognition: Juxtaposing Perspectives on National Socialism." *Beyond the Conceivable: Studies on Germany, Nazism, and the Holocaust*. Berkeley, Calif.: University of California Press.

———. 2000b. "Knowledge of Expansion: On the Geopolitics of Karl Haushofer." In *Beyond the Conceivable: Studies on Germany, Nazism, and the Holocaust*. Berkeley, Calif.: University of California Press.

———. 2000c. "Norms of Domination: Nazi Legal Concepts of World Order." In *Beyond the Conceivable: Studies on Germany, Nazism, and the Holocaust*. Berkeley, Calif.: University of California Press.

Doray, Bertrand. 1981. *Le Taylorisme, une folie rationnelle?* Paris: Dunod.

Dreschler, Horst. 1986. *Le Sud-Ouest africain sous la domination allemande: la lutte des Hereros et des Namas contre l'impérialisme allemand 1884–1915*. East Berlin: Akademie Verlag.

Drieu la Rochelle, Pierre. 1949. *Gilles*. Paris: Gallimard.

Drouard, Alain. 1992. *Alexis Carrel et la Fondation Française pour l'Étude des Problèmes Humains*. Paris: Editions de la Maison des Sciences de l'Homme.

Drumont, Edouard. 1986. *La France juive*. 2 vols. Paris: La librairie française.

Dupeux, Luis. 1992. " 'Révolution conservatrice' et hitlérisme: Etude sur la nature de l'hitlérisme." In Luis Dupeux, ed., *La Révolution conservatrice" dans l'Allemagne de Weimar*. Paris: Kimé.

Eksteins, Modris. 2000. *Rites of Spring: The Great War and the Birth of the Modern Age*. London: Macmillan.

Elias, Norbert. 1973–75. *La Civilisation des moeurs et la dynamique de l'Occident*. Paris: Calmann-Lévy. Translation of *Über den Prozess der Zivilisation* (Frankfurt: Suhrkamp, 1969).

———. 1996. *The Germans, Power Struggles and the Development of Habitus in the Nineteenth and Twentieth Centuries*. Cambridge, England: Polity Press.

Ellis, John. 1975. *The Social History of the Machine Gun*. New York: Pantheon.

Etemad, Bouda. 2001. *La Possession du monde: Poids et mésures de la colonisation*. Brussels: Complexe.

Evans, Richard J. 1987. *Death in Hamburg: Society and Politics in the Cholera Years, 1890–1910*. Oxford: Clarendon Press.

———. 1992. "Epidemics and Revolutions: Cholera in Nineteenth-Century Europe." In Terence Ranger and Paul Slack, eds., *Epidemics and Ideas: Essays on the Historical Perception of Pestilence*. Cambridge, England: Cambridge University Press.

Evard, Jean-Luc. 1996. "Ernst Jünger et les juifs." *Les Temps modernes*, no. 589.

Field, Geoffrey G. 1981. *Evangelist of Race: The Germanic Vision of Houston Stewart Chamberlain*. New York: Columbia University Press.

Finchelstein, Federico. 1999a. *Los Alemanes, el Holocausto y la culpa colectiva: El debate Goldhagen*. Buenos Aires: Eudeba.

———. 1999b. "Revisitando el *Sonderweg* aleman: Los historiadores, la tradicion de la derecha y la ruta historica de Bismark a Hitler." In Patricio Geli, ed., *La derecha politica en la historia europea contemporanea*. Buenos Aires: Eudeba.

Ford, Henry. 1941. *Der internationale Jude*. Leipzig: Hammer Verlag. Translation of "The International Jew" in the *Dearborn* [Michigan] *Independent*, 1918. Reprint, CPA Book Publisher, Oregon.

Foucault, Michel. 1975 *Surveiller et punir: Naissance de la prison*. Paris: Gallimard. English translation, *Discipline and Punish: The Birth of the Prison* (Harmondsworth, England: Penguin Books, 1991).

Friedlander, Henry. 1997. *Der Weg zur NZ-Genozid*. Berlin: Berlin Verlag. Translation of *The Origins of Nazi Gevoado: From Euthanasia to the Final Solution* (Chapel Hill, N.C.: University of North Carolina Press, 1995).

Friedländer, Saul. 1993. "Martin Broszat and the Historicization of National-Socialism." In *Memory, History, and the Extermination of the Jews of Europe*. Bloomington: Indiana University Press.

———. 1997. *Nazi Germany and the Jews*. Vol. I, *The Years of Persecution, 1933–1939*. New York: HarperCollins.

Furet, François. 1999. *The Passing of an Illusion: Essay on the Communist Idea in the Twentieth Century*. Chicago: University of Chicago Press.

Furet, François, and Ernst Nolte. 2001. *Fascism and Communism*. Lincoln: University of Nebraska Press.

Fussell, Paul. 1975. *The Great War and Modern Memory*. Oxford: Oxford University Press.

Garland, David. 1990. *Punishment and Modern Society*. Oxford: Oxford University Press.

Gaudemar, Jean-Paul de. 1982. *L'Ordre et la production: Naissance et formes de la discipline d'usine*. Paris: Dunod.

Gay, Peter. 1993. *The Cultivation of Hatred*. New York: Norton.

Gerould, Daniel C. 1992. *Guillotine, Its Legend and Lore*. New York: Blast Books.

Gibelli, Antonio. 1991. *L'officina della Guerra: la Grande Guerra e le transformazioni del mondo mentale*. Turin: Bollati-Boringhieri.

Gide, André. 1996. *Journal I. 1887–1925*, Paris: Gallimard.

Gilman, Sander. 1991. *The Jew's Body*. New York: Routledge.

Ginzburg, Carlo. 1986. "Spie: Radici di un paradigma indiziario." In *Miti, emblemi, spie: morfologia e storia*, Turin: Einaudi.

Goebbels, Joseph. 1971. "Berlin, Opernplatz: Bücherverbrennung auf der Kundgebung der deutschen Studenterschaft wider den undeutschen Geist." *Reden, 1932–1939*. Vol. 1. Düsseldorf: Droste.

Goldhagen, Daniel J. 1996. *Hitler's Willing Executioners: Ordinary Germans and the Holocaust*. London: Little, Brown.

Graml, Hermann. 1993. "Rassismus und Lebensraum: Völkermord im zweiten Weltkrieg." In Karl-Dietrich Bracher, Manfred Funke, and Hans-Adolf Jacobsen, eds., *Deutschland 1933–1945: neue Studien zur nationalsozialistischen Herrschaft*. Düsseldorf: Droste.

Gramsci, Antonio. 1975. "Americanismo e fordismo." 1934. In *Quaderni del carcere*. 4 vols. Turin: Enaudi.

Grant, Madison. 1920. *The Passing of the Great Race or the Racial Basis of European History*. 1916. Reprint, London: G. Bell and Sons.

Grenville, J. A. S. 1964. *Lord Salisbury and Foreign Policy: The Close of the Nineteenth Century*. London: Athlona Press.

Gross, Raphael. 2000. *Carl Schmitt und die Juden*. Frankfurt: Suhrkamp.

Gumplowicz, Ludwig. 1973. *Der Rassenkampf*. 1883. Reprint, Innsbruck: Scientia Verlag.

Habermas, Jürgen. 1987a. "Eine Art Schadensabwicklung." In *Historikerstreit*. Munich: Piper. French translation, "Une manière de liquider les dommages." *Devant l'histoire: les documents de la controverse sur la singularité de l'extermination des juifs par le régime nazi* (Paris: Editions du Cerf, 1988).

———. 1987b. "Geschichtsbewußtsein und posttraditionale Identität: Die Westorientierung der Bundesrepublik." In *Eine Art Schadensabwicklung: Kleine politische Schriften*. Vol. 6. Frankfurt: Suhrkamp. French translation, "Conscience historique et identité post-traditionnelle," in *Ecrits politiques* (Paris: Editions du Cerf, 1990).

———. 1997. "Geschichte ist ein Teil von Uns." *Die Zeit*, no. 12.

Hake, Sabine. 1998. "Mapping the Native Body: On Africa and the Colonial Film in the Third Reich." In Sara Friedrichsmayer, Sara Lennox, and Susañne Zantop, eds., *The Imperialist Imagination: German Colonialism and Its Legacy*. Ann Arbor: University of Michigan Press.

Hamann, Brigitte. 1996. *Hitlers Wien: Lehrjahre eines Diktators*. Munich: Piper.

Hamon, A. 1895. *Psychologie de l'anarchiste socialiste*. Paris: Stock.

Hart, R. C. 1911. "A Vindication of War." *The Nineteenth Century and After*, no. 70.

Haushofer, Karl. 1936. "Geopolitische Grundlagen." *Grundlagen, Aufbau und Wirtschaftsordnung des nationalsozialistischen Staates*. Berlin.

———. 1986. "La Vie des frontières politiques." 1930. Reprinted in *De la géopolitique* (Paris: Fayard).

Hayes, Carlton J. 1940. "The Novelty of Totalitarianism in the History of Western Civilization." *Proceedings of the American Philosophical Society* 82.

Hecht, Jennifer Michael. 2000. "Vacher de la Pouge and the Rise of Nazi Science." *Journal of the History of Ideas*, 61, no. 2.

Heer, Hannes. 1995. "Die Logik der Vernichtung: Wehrmacht und Partisanenkampf." In Hannes Heer and Klaus Naumann, eds., *Vernichtungskrieg: Verbrechen der Wehrmacht 1941–1945*. Hamburg: Hamburger Edition.

Helbig, Ludwig. 1988. "Der koloniale Frühfaschismus." In Nangolo Mbumba and Helgand Patemann, eds., *Ein Land, eine Zukunft*. Wuppertal: Peter Hammer.

Herbert, Ulrich, and William Templer. 1997. *Hitler's Foreign Workers*. Cambridge, England: Cambridge University Press.

Herf, Jeffrey. 1984. *Reactionary Modernism: Technology, Culture, and Politics in Weimar and the Third Reich*. Cambridge, England: Cambridge University Press.

Hilberg, Raul. 1985. *The Destruction of the European Jews*. New York and London:

Holmes & Meier. French translation, *La Destruction des juifs d'Europe* (Paris: Fayard, 1988).

Hillgruber, Andreas. 1986. *Zweierlei Untergang: die Zerschlagung des deutschen Reiches und das Ende des europäischen Judentums.* Berlin: Siedler.

Hitler, Adolf. 1943. *Mein Kampf.* 1925 and 1927. Reprint, Munich: Franz Eher.

———. 1952. *Libres propos sur la guerre et la paix recueillis sur l'ordre de Martin Bormann.* 2 vols. Paris: Flammarion.

Hobsbawm, Eric J. 1994. *Age of Extremes: The Short Twentieth Century, 1914–1991.* London.

———. 1997. "Barbarism: A User's Guide." *On History,* pp. 253–65. London: Weidenfeld & Nicolson.

Hochschild, Adam. 1998. *Les Fantômes du Roi Léopold II: Un holocauste oublié.* Paris: Balland. Translation of *King Leopold's Ghost* (Boston: Houghton Mifflin, 1998).

Hofstadter, Richard. 1992. *Social Darwinism in American Thought.* 1944. Reprint, Boston: Beacon Press.

Holz, Klaus. 2001. *Nationaler Antisemitismus: Wissenssoziologie einer Weltanschauung.* Hamburg: Hamburger Edition.

Horne, John. 1994. "Les Mains coupées: 'Atrocités allemandes' et opinion française en 1914." In Jean-Jacques Becker, ed., *Guerre et cultures 1914–1918.* Paris: Armand Colin.

Howard, Michael. 1988. *La Guerre dans l'histoire de l'Occident.* Paris: Fayard.

Hüppauf, Bernd. 1993. "Schlachtenmythen und die Konstruktion des 'Neuen Menschen.'" In Gerhard Hirschfeld, Gerd Krumeich, and Irina Renz, eds., *Keiner fühlt sich hier mehr als Mensch: Erlebnis und Wirkung des ersten Weltkrieges.* Essen: Klartext.

———. 1997. "Modernity and Violence: Observations Concerning a Contradictory Relationship." In Bernd Hüppauf, ed., *War, Violence, and the Modern Condition.* Berlin: Walter de Gruyter.

Husson, Edouard. 2000. *Comprendre Hitler et la Shoah: Les Historiens de la République Fédérale d'Allemagne et l'identité allemande depuis 1949.* Paris: Presses Universitaires de France.

Ignatieff, Michael. 1978. *A Just Measure of Pain: The Penitentiary in the Industrial Revolution, 1750–1850.* New York: Pantheon.

Isnenghi, Mario. 1970. *Il mito della Grande Guerra da Marinetti a Malaparte.* Bari: Laterza.

Israel, Giorgio, and Giorgio Nastasi. 1998. *Scienza e razza nell'Italia fascista.* Bologna: Il Mulino.

Jäckel, Eberhard. 1973. *Hitlers Weltanschauung.* Stuttgart: DVA. French translation, *Hitler idéologue,* (Paris: Calmann-Levy, 1973; reprint, Paris: Folio-Gallimard, 1974).

Jacobsen, Hans-Adolf. 1979. *Karl Haushofer: Leben und Werk.* Boppart am Rehin: Boldt.

Jahn, Peter. 1991. "'Russenfurcht' und Antibolschewismus: zur Enstehung und Wirkung von Feindbildern." In *Erobern und Vernichten: der Krieg gegen die Sowjetunion 1941–1945.* Berlin: Argon.

Jones, William David. 1999. *The Lost Debate: German Socialist Intellectuals and To-talitarianism.* Urbana and Chicago: University of Illinois University Press.

Jünger, Ernst. 1930. "Über Nationalismus und Judenfrage." *Süddeutsche Monat-shefte,* no. 27.

———. 1980a. *Journaux de guerre.* Paris: Christian Bourgeois. Translation of *Tage-bücher, vol. 2* (Stuttgart: Klett-Cotta, 1963).

———. 1980b. *L'Etat universel suivi de la mobilisation totale.* Paris: Gallimard. French translation of *Die totale Mobilmachung* (Berlin: 1930).

———. 1989. *Le Travailleur.* Paris: Christian Bourgeois. French translation of *Der Arbeiter* (Berlin: 1932).

———. 1997. *La Guerre comme experience intérieure.* Paris: Christian Bourgeois. French translation of *Der Kampf als inneres Erlebnis* (Stuttgart: Klett-Cotta, 1980).

Kafka, Franz. 1952. "In der Strafkolonie." 1919. In *Erzählungen.* Frankfurt: Fischer. French translation, "A la colonie pénitentiaire," in *Un artiste de la faim et autres récits* (Paris: Gallimard, 1990).

Kantorowicz, Ernst. 1957. *The King's Two Bodies.* Princeton: Princeton University Press.

Keegan, John. 1978. *The Face of Battle.* Harmondsworth: Penguin Books.

Kenz, Peter. 1992. "Pogroms and White Ideology in the Russian Civil War." In John D. Klier and Shlomo Lambrosa, eds., *Pogroms: Anti-Jewish Violence in Modern Russian History.* Cambridge: Cambridge University Press.

Kern, Stephen. 1983. *The Culture of Time and Space 1880–1918,* Cambridge, Mass.: Harvard University Press.

Kershaw, Ian. 1998. *Hitler 1889–1936.* London: Allen Lane.

———. 2000. *Hitler 1936–1945.* London: Allen Lane.

Kevles, David J. 1985. *In the Name of Eugenics: Genetics and the Uses of Human Heredity.* New York: Knopf.

Kidd, Benjamin. 1894. *Social Evolution.* New York: Macmillan.

Killingray, David. 1989. "Colonial Warfare in West Africa." In J. A. de Moor and H. L. Wesseling, eds., *Colonialism and War: Essays on Colonial Wars in Asia and Africa.* Leiden: E. J. Brill/Universitaire Pers Leiden.

King, David 1972. *Trotsky.* London: Penguin Books.

Klee, Ernst. 1983. *"Euthanasie" im NS-Staat: Die "Vernichtung lebensunwerten Lebens."* Frankfurt: Fischer.

Koch, Hans-Joachim. 1973. *Der Sozial-Darwinismus.* Munich: C. H. Beck.

Kohn, Hans. 1948. "The Totalitarian Philosophy of War." *Proceedings of the Ameri-can Philosophical Society,* 82.

Korinman, Michel. 1999. *Deutschland über Alles: le pangermanisme 1890–1945.* Paris: Fayard.

Korsch, Karl. 1942. "Notes on History: The Ambiguities of Totalitarian Ideologies." *New Essays* 6, no. 2.

Kracauer, Siegfried. 1947. *From Caligari to Hitler: A Psychological History of German Film.* Princeton: Princeton University Press.

———. 1960. *Theory of Film: The Redemption of Physical Reality.* Oxford and New York: Oxford University Press.

Krüger, Gesine. 1999. *Kriegsbewältigung und Geschichtsbewusstsein: Realität, Deu-*

*tung und Verarbeitung des deutschen Kolonialkriegs in Namibia 1904 bis 1907.* Göttingen: Vandenhoeck & Ruprecht.

Krumeich, Gerd. 1994. "La Place de la guerre de 1914–1918 dans l'histoire culturelle de l'Allemagne." In Jean-Jacques Becker, ed., *Guerre et cultures 1914–1918.* Paris: Armand Colin.

Kühl, Stefan. 1994. *The Nazi Connection: Eugenics, American Racism, and German National-Socialism.* Oxford and New York: Oxford University Press.

Kuklick, Henrika. 1991. *The Savage Within: The Social History of British Anthropology 1885–1945.* Cambridge, England: Cambridge University Press.

Labanca, Nicola. 1999. "Il razzismo coloniale italiano." In Alberto Burgio, ed., *Nel nome della razza: Il rassismo nella storia d'Italia 1870–1945.* Bologna: Il Mulino.

Lal, Vinay, and Omer Bartov. 1998. "Genocide, Barbaric Others, and the Violence of Categories: A Response to Omer Bartov" and "Reply." In *American Historical Review* 5, no. 103.

Landes, David S. 2000. *Richesse et pauvreté des nations.* Paris: Albin Michel. Translation of *The Wealth and Poverty of Nations* (New York: Norton, 1998).

Lange, Karl. 1965. "Der Terminus 'Lebensraum' in Adolf Hitler's *Mein Kampf.*" *Vierteljahreshefte für Zeitgeschichte,* no 13.

Lanzmann, Claude. 1985. *Shoah.* Paris: Fayard.

La Vergata, Antonello. 1990. *L'equilibrio e la guerra della natura: Dalla teologia naturale al darwinismo.* Naples: Morano.

Le Bon, Gustave. 1912. "Psychologie de la révolution française." *Revue bleue: Revue politique et littéraire.*

———. 1919. *Lois psychologiques de l'évolution des peoples.* Paris: Alcan.

———. 1995. *La Psychologie des foules.* 1895. Reprint, Paris: Presses Universitaires de France.

Le Cour Grandmaison, Olivier. 2001. "Quand Tocqueville légitimisait les boucheries." *Le Monde diplomatique: Manière de voir,* no. 58.

Lee, Richard. 1864. "The Extinction of the Races." *Journal of the Anthropological Society.* London: Trübner & Co.

Leed, Eric J. 1979. *No Man's Land: Combat and Identity in World War I.* Cambridge, England: Cambridge University Press.

Leibbrandt, Gottlieb. 1939. *Bolschewismus und Abendland: Idee und Geschichte eines Kampfes gegen Europa.* Berlin: Junker & Dünnhaupt.

Lenger, Friedrich. 1954. *Werner Sombart 1863–1941.* Munich: C. H. Beck.

Leroy-Beaulieu, Anatole. 1893. *Israël chez les nations.* Paris: Calmann-Lévy.

Leslie, Esther. 2000. *Walter Benjamin: Overpowering Conformism.* London: Pluto Press.

Levi, Primo. 1988. *The Drowned and the Saved.* London: Michael Joseph.

Lidsky, Paul. 1982. *Les Écrivains contre la Commune.* Paris: Maspero,

Lindqvist, Sven. 1998. *Exterminez toutes ces brutes: L'Odyssée d'un homme au coeur de la nuit et les origines du genocide européen.* Paris: Le Serpent à Plumes. French translation of *Ultrota varenda jävel* (Stockholm: Albert Bonniers Förlag AB, 1992). English translation, *"Exterminate All the Brutes"* (New York: The New Press, 1996).

Lombroso, Cesare. 1887. *L'Homme criminel.* Paris: Alcan. French translation of *L'uomo delinquente* (Turin: 1876).

Lombroso, Cesare, and Roberto Laschi. 1890. *Il delitto politico e le revoluzioni.* Turin: Bocca.

Lorimer, Douglas A. 1978. *Colour, Class and the Victorians: English Attitudes to the Negro in the Mid-Nineteenth Century.* New York: Leicester University Press and Holmes & Meier.

Losurdo, Domenico. 1991. "Marx et l'histoire du totalitarisme." In Jacques Bidet and Jacques Texier, eds., *Fin du communisme?* Paris: Presses Universitaires de Frances.

———. 1996. *Il revisionismo storico: Problemi e miti.* Bari and Rome: Laterza.

Löwy, Michael. 1993. "Fire Alarm: Walter Benjamin's Critique of Technology." In *On Changing the World: Essays in Political Philosophy from Karl Marx to Walter Benjamin.* Atlantic Highlands, N.J.: Humanities Press.

———. 2001. "La dialettica della civiltà: Figure della barbaria moderna nel XX secolo." In Marcello Flores, ed., *Storia, verità, giustizia: I crimini del XX secolo.* Milan: Mondadori.

Lukàcs, Georg. 1984. *Die Zerstörung der Vernunft: Der Weg des Irrationalismus von Schelling bis Hitler.* Berlin: Aufbau Verlag.

Lüsebrink, Hans-Jürgen. 1989. " 'Tirailleurs sénégalais' und 'schwarze Schande': Verlaufsformen und Konsequenzen einer deutschfranzösischen Auseinandersetzung." In Janos Riez and Joachim Schultz, eds., *Tirailleurs sénégalais.* Frankfurt: Lang.

Madajzyk, Czeslaw 1993. "Vom 'Generalplan Ost' zum 'Generalsiedlungsplan.' " In Mechtild Rössler and Sabine Schleiermacher, eds., *Der "Generalplan Ost": Hauptlinien der nationalsozialistischen Planungs- und Vernichtungspolitik.* Berlin: Akademie Verlag.

Maier, Charles. 1978. "Entre le taylorisme et la technocratie: Idéologies et conceptions de la productivité industrielle dans l'Europe des années 1920." *Recherches,* no. 32–33, pp. 95–134.

———. 1997. "Secolo corto o epoca lunga? L'unità storica dell'età industriale e le transformazioni della territorialità." In Claudio Pavone, ed., *'900: I tempi della storia,* pp. 29–56. Rome: Donzelli

Maier, Hans. 2001. "Potentials for Violence in the Nineteenth Century: Technology of War, Colonialism, 'the People in Arms.' " *Totalitarian Movements and Political Religions* 2, no. 1.

Maistre, Joseph de. 1979. "Les Soirées de Saint-Pétersbourg." In *Oeuvres complètes de Joseph de Maistre.* Librairie Catholique Emmanuel Vitte, Lyons-Paris, 1884–1887. Reprint, Geneva: Slatkine, vol. 4.

Mandel, Ernest. 1986. *The Meaning of the Second World War.* London: Verso.

Mann, Thomas. 1981. *Tagebücher 1918–1921.* Frankfurt: Fischer. French translation, *Journal 1918–1923* (Paris: Gallimard, 1985).

Marestang, M. 1892. "La Dépopulation aux îles Marquises." *Revue scientifique* 44.

Marinetti, Filippo Tommaso. 1909. "Manifeste futuriste." *Le Figaro,* 20 February.

Marx, Karl. 1938. *Capital.* London: George Allen & Unwin. English translation of *Das Kapital* (Berlin: 1867; reprint, Berlin: Dietz Verlag, 1975, 3 vols.).

Marx, Karl, and Friedrich Engels. 1998. *The Communist Manifesto.* 1848. Reprint, London and New York: Verso.

Maspero, François. 1993. *L'Honneur de Saint-Artaud.* Paris: Plon.

Massin, Benoît. 1993. "Anthropologie raciale et national-socialisme: Heurs et malheurs des paradigmes de la race." In J. Olff-Nathan, ed., *La Science sous le Troisième Reich.* Paris: Seuil.

Mayer, Arno J. 1971. *Dynamics of Counterrevolution in Europe 1870–1956: An Analytic Framework.* New York: Harper & Row.

————. 1981. *The Persistence of the Old Regime.* New York: Pantheon.

————. 1988. *Why Did the Heavens Not Darken? The "Final Solution" in History.* New York: Pantheon.

————. 2000. *The Furies: Violence and Terror in the French and Russian Revolutions.* Princeton: Princeton University Press.

Meige, Henry. 1893. "Le Juif errant à la Salpêtrière." *Nouvelle iconographie de la Salpêtrière* 6.

Melossi, Dario, and Massimo Pavarini. 1997. *Carcere e fabbrica: Alle origini del sistema penitenziario, XVI–XIX secolo,* Bologna: Il Mulino.

Miccoli, Giovanni. 1997. "Santa Sede, questione ebraica e antisemitismo." *Storia d'Italia: Annali 11, Gli ebrei in Italia.* Vol. 2. Turin: Einaudi.

Michaud, Eric. 1996. *Un art d'éternité: L'Image et le temps du national-socialisme.* Paris: Gallimard.

Michels, Robert. 1971. *Les Parties politiques.* Paris: Flammarion.

Mill, John Stuart. 1991. *On Liberty and Other Essays.* Oxford: Oxford University Press.

Milza, Pierre. 1999. *Mussolini,* Paris: Fayard.

Mitzman, Arthur. 1973. *Sociology and Estrangement: Three Sociologists of Imperial Germany.* New York: Knopf.

Mommsen, Hans. 1983. "Die Realisierung des Utopischen: Die 'Endlösung' der Judenfrage im 'Dritten Reich,' " *Geschichte und Gesellschaft,* no. 1.

Moriani, Giovanni. 1999. *Il secolo dell'odio: Conflitti razziali e di classe nel novecento.* Venice: Marsilio.

Mosca, Gaetano. 1972. *La Classe politica.* Bari and Rome: Laterza.

Moscovici, Serge. 1985. *L'Âge des foules.* Brussels: Complexe.

Mosse, George L. 1964. *The Crisis of German Ideology: The Cultural Origins of the Third Reich.* New York: Grosset & Dunlap.

————. 1974. *The Nationalization of the Masses: Political Symbolism and Mass Movements in Germany from the Napoleonic Wars Through the Third Reich.* New York: Howard Fertig.

————. 1978. *Toward the Final Solution: A History of European Racism.* New York: Howard Fertig.

————. 1990. *Fallen Soldiers: Reshaping the Memory of the World Wars.* Oxford and New York: Oxford University Press.

————. 1999. *The Fascist Revolution.* New York: Howard Fertig.

Mucchieli, Laurent. 1998. *La Découverte du social: Naissance de la sociologie en France (1870–1914).* Paris: La Découverte.

Müller, Filip. 1980. *Trois ans dans une chambre à gaz d'Auschwitz.* Paris: Pygmalion. French translation of *Sonderbehandlung: Drei Jahre in den Kremmatorien und Gaskammern von Auschwitz* (Munich, 1979).

Neocleous, Mark. 1997. *Fascism*. Buckingham, England: Open University Press.

Neumann, Franz. 1987. *Behemoth: Theory and Practice of National-Socialism*. Oxford and New York: Oxford University Press.

Noaks, Jeremy. 1984. "Nazism and Eugenics: The Background to the Nazi Sterilization Law of 14 July 1933." In R. J. Bullen, H. Pogge von Strandmann, and B. Polonsky, eds., *Ideas into Politics: Aspects of European History 1880–1950*. London: Barnes & Noble.

Nolte, Ernst. 1993. *Forever in the Shadow of Hitler? Original Documents of the Historikerstreit*. Atlantic Highlands, N.J.: Humanities Press.

————. 2000. *La Guerre civile européenne 1917–1945: National-socialisme et bolshevisme*. Paris: Editions des Syrtes. French translation of *Der europäische Bürgerkrieg: Nationalsozialismus und Bolschewismus 1917–1945* (Berlin and Frankfurt: Propyläen/Ullstein, 1987).

Norton Cru, Jean. 1982. *Du témoignage*. Paris: Allia.

Novicow, Jacques. 1910. *La Critique du darwinisme social*. Paris: Alcan.

Nye, Robert Allen. 1975. *The Origins of Crowd Psychology*. London: Sage Publications.

————. 1984. *Crime, Madness, and Politics in Modern France: The Medical Concept of National Decline*. Princeton: Princeton University Press.

O'Brian, Patricia 1982. *The Promise of Punishment: Prisons in Nineteenth-Century France*. Princeton: Princeton University Press.

Panoff, Michel. 1992. "Le Darwinisme social à l'oeuvre en Océanie insulaire." In Patrick Tort, ed., *Darwinisme et société*. Paris: Presses Universitaires de France.

Papini, Giovanni. 1913. "La vita non è sacra." *Lacerba* 1, no. 20.

Parekh, Bhikhu. 1995. "Liberalism and Colonialism: A Critique of Locke and Mill." In Jan Nederveen Pieterse and Bhikhu Parekh, eds., *The Decolonization of Imagination: Culture, Knowledge and Power*. London: Zed Books.

Pareto, Vilfredo. 1965. *Les Systèmes socialistes*. 1902. Reprint, Geneva: Droz.

Parker, Geoffrey. 1988. *The Military Revolution: Military Innovation and the Rise of the West*. Cambridge and New York: Cambridge University Press.

Perrier, Edmond. 1888. *Le Transformisme*. Paris: Baillière.

Perrot, Michelle. 2001. *Les Ombres de l'histoire: Crime et châtiment au XIXe siècle*. Paris: Flammarion.

Peukert, Detlev. 1987. *Inside Nazi Germany: Conformity, Opposition and Racism in Everyday Life*. London: Penguin Books.

Pichot, André. 2000. *La Société pure: De Darwin à Hitler*. Paris: Flammarion.

Pick, Daniel. 1989. *Faces of Degeneration: A European Disorder 1848–1918*. Cambridge, England: Cambridge University Press.

————. 1993. *War Machine: The Rationalization of Slaughter in the Modern Age*. New Haven and London: Yale University Press.

Picker, Henry. 1977. *Hitlers Tischgespräche im Führerhauptquartier*. Stuttgart: Seewald Verlag. Translation of *Hitler's Secret Conversations* (New York: Farrar, Straus & Giroux, 1953).

Pogliano, Claudio. 1984. "Scienza e stripe: Eugenica in Italia (1912–1939)." *Passato e Presente*, no. 5.

————. 1999. "Eugenisti ma con giudizio." In Alberto Burgio, ed., *Nel nome della razza: Il razzismo nella storia d'Italia 1870–1945.* Bologna: Il Mulino.

Pois, Robert A. 1993. *La Réligion de la nature et le national-socialisme.* Paris: Editions du Cerf. French translation of *National Socialism and the Religion of Nature* (London: Croom, 1986).

Poliakov, Léon. 1981. *Histoire de l'antisémitisme.* 2 vols. Paris: Calmann-Lévy.

Pollack, Michael. 1989. "Une politique scientifique: Le concours de l'anthropologie, de la biologie et du droit." In François Bédarida, ed., *La Politique nazi d'extermination.* Paris: Albin Michel.

Postone, Moishe. 1988. "Nationalsozialismus and Antisemitismus: Ein theoretischer Versuch." In Dan Diner, ed., *Zivilisationsbruch: Denken nach Auschwitz.* Frankfurt: Fischer.

Pouget, Michel. 1998. *Taylor et le taylorisme.* Paris: Presses Universitaires de France.

Pressac, Jean-Claude. 1993. *Les Crématoires d'Auschwitz: La Machinerie du meurtre de masse.* Paris: CNRS Editions.

Proal, Louis. 1898. *La Criminalité politique.* Paris: Alcan.

Procacci, Giovanna. 2000. *Soldati e prigionieri italiani nella Grande Guerra.* Turin: Bollati Boringhieri.

Proctor, Robert. 1988. *Racial Hygiene: Medicine Under the Nazis.* Cambridge, Mass. Harvard University Press.

————. 1999. *The Nazi War on Cancer.* Princeton: Princeton University Press.

Rabinbach, Anson. 1978. "L'Esthétique de la production sous le Troisième Reich." *Recherches,* no. 32–33.

————. 1992. *The Human Motor: Energy, Fatigue, and the Origins of Modernity.* Berkeley: University of California Press.

Rainger, Ronald. 1978. "Race, Politics, and Science: The Anthropological Society of London in the 1860s." *Victorian Studies,* no. 1.

Ratzel, Friedrich. 1966. *Lebensraum: Eine biogeographische Studie.* 1901. Reprint, Darmstadt: Wissenschaftliche Buchgesellschaft.

Reade, William Winwood. 1863. *Savage Africa.* London: Smith, Eldon & Co.

Reemtsma, Jan Philipp. 1995. "Die Idee des Vernichtungskrieges." In Hannes Heer and Klaus Naumann, eds., *Vernichtungskrieg: Verbrechen der Wehrmacht 1941 bis 1944,* pp. 377–401. Hamburg: Hamburger Edition.

Reichel, Peter. 1993. *La Fascination du nazisme.* Paris: Odile Jacob. French translation of *Der schöne Schein des Dritten Reiches* (Munich: Hanser Verlag, 1991).

Reuth, Ralf Georg. 1990. *Goebbels: Eine Biographie.* Munich: Piper.

Revelli, Marco. 2001. *Oltre il Novecento: La politica, le ideologie e le insidie del lavoro.* Turin: Einaudi.

Richard, Lionel. 1995. *L'Art et la guerre: Les Artistes confrontés à la seconde guerre mondiale.* Paris: Flammarion.

Rivet, Daniel. 1992. "Le Fait colonial et nous: Histoire d'un éloignement." *Vingtième siècle,* no. 33.

Rochat, Giorgio. 1980. "Il genocidio cirenaico." *Belfagor* 35, no. 4.

Rosenberg, Alfred. 1922. *Pest in Russland.* Munich.

————. 1986. *Le Mythe du vingtième siècle.* Paris: Avalon.

Rousso, Henry. 2001. "Juger le passé? Justice et histoire en France." In *Vichy: L'Événement, la mémoire, l'histoire*. Paris: Folio-Gallimard.

Ruche, Georg, and Otto Kirchheimer. 1994. *Peine et structure sociale*. Reprint, Paris: Editions du Cerf. English translation, *Punishment and Social Structure* (New York: 1939).

Ruffié, J., and J. C. Sournia. 1993. *Les Épidémies dans l'histoire de l'homme: De la peste au Sida*, Paris: Flammarion.

Said, Edward. 1980. *L'orientalisme: L'Orient créé par l'Occident*. Paris: Seuil. French translation of *Orientalism* (New York: Knopf, 1978).

————. 1993. *Culture and Imperialism*. London: Chatto & Windus.

Salvati, Mariuccia. 2001. *Novecento: Interpretazioni e bilanci*. Bari and Rome: Laterza.

Sartre, Jean-Paul. 1954. *Réflexions sur la question juive*. 1946. Reprint, Paris: Gallimard.

Schmitt, Carl. 1933. "Das gute Recht der deutschen Revolution." *West-Deutscher Beobachter*, 12 March.

————. 1936. *Das Judentum in der Rechtswissenschaft: Ansprachen, Vorträge und Ergebnisse der Tagung der Rechtsgruppe Hochschullehrer des NRSB am 3. und 4. Oktober 1936*. Berlin.

————. 1974. *Der Nomos der Erde im Völkerrecht des Jus Publicum Europaeum. 1950*. Reprint, Berlin: Duncker & Humblot.

————. 1982. *Der Leviathan in der Staatslehre des Thomas Hobbes: Sinn und Fehlschlag eines politischen Symbols*. 1938. Reprint, Köln-Lövenich: Hohenheim Verlag.

————. 1988a. "Totaler Feind, totaler Krieg, totaler Staat." 1937. In *Positionen und Begriffe im Kampf mit Weimar-Genf-Versailles 1923–1939*. Berlin: Duncker & Humblot.

————. 1988b. "Grossraum gegen Universalismus: Der Völkerrechtliche Kampf und die Monroedoktrin." 1939. In *Positionen und Begriffe im Kampf mit Weimar-Genf-Versailles 1923–1939*. Berlin: Duncker & Humblot.

————. 1991. *Völkerrechtliche Grossraumordnung*. 1941. Reprint, Berlin: Duncker & Humblot.

————. 1993. *Über die drei Arten des rechtswissenschaftlichen Denkens*. 1934. Reprint, Berlin: Duncker & Humblot.

————. 1996. *Der Begriff des Politischen*. 1932. Reprint, Berlin: Dunker & Humblot. French translation, *La Notion de politique* (Paris: Flammarion, 1992).

Schor, Ralph. 1989. "Le Paris des libertés." In André Kaspi and Antoine Marès, eds., *Le Paris des étrangers*. Paris: Imprimerie nationale.

Schulte, Christoph. 1996. "Dégénérescence et sionisme." In Delphine Bechtel, Jacques Le Rider, and Dominique Bourel, eds., *Max Nordau 1849–1923*. Paris: Editions Cerf.

Sellier, André. 1998. *Histoire du camp de Dora*. Paris: La Découverte.

Siebert, Theodor. 1941. "Der jüdische Feind." *Völkischer Beobachter*. November 12.

Sighele, Scipio. 1985. *La folla delinquente*. Venice: Marsilio. French translation, *La Foule criminelle: Essai de psychologie collective* (Paris: Alcan, 1992).

Simmel, Georg. 1987. *Philosophie de l'argent*. Paris: Presses Universitaires de France. Translation of *Philosophie des Geldes* (1900; reprint, Berlin: Duncker & Humblot, 1977).

Simpson, Louis. 1965. *The Poetry of War 1939–1945*. New York: Harcourt, Brace & World.

Sinclair, Upton. 1985. *The Jungle*. 1906. Reprint, Harmondsworth, England: Penguin Books.

Siva, P. 1920. "La rivoluzione mondiale e gli ebrei." *Civiltà cattolica*, no. 73.

Smith, Woodruff D. 1986. *The Ideological Origins of Nazi Imperialism*. Oxford and New York: Oxford University Press.

Sofsky, Wolfgang. 1995. *L'Organisation de la terreur: Les Camps de concentration*. Paris: Calmann-Lévy. Translated from *Die Odnung des Terrors: Das Konzentrationslager* (Frankfurt: Fischer, 1993).

———. 1998. *Traité de la violence*. Paris: Gallimard. French translation of *Traktat über die Gewalt* (Frankfurt: Fischer, 1996).

Sombart, Werner. 1913. *Der Bourgeois: Zur Geistesgeschichte des modernen Wirtschaftsmenschen*. 1912. Leipzig: Duncker & Humblot.

———. 1920. *Die Juden und das Wirtschaftsleben*. Leipzig: Duncker & Humblot.

Sontag, Susan. 1993. *La Maladie comme métaphore*. Paris: Christian Bourgeois. French translation of *Illness as Metaphor* (New York: Farrar, Straus & Giroux, 1977).

Spengler, Oswald. 1993. *Der Untergang des Abendlandes*. 1923. Reprint, Munich: Deutscher Toschenbuch Verlag.

Spierenburg, Pietr. 1984. *The Spectacle of Suffering: Executions and the Evolution of Repression*. Cambridge, England: Cambridge University Press.

Stannard, David E. 1992. *American Holocaust: The Conquest of the New World*. Oxford and New York: Oxford University Press.

Stark, Johannes, and Wilhelm Müller. 1941. *Jüdische und deutsche Physik*. Leipzig: Helingsche Verlagsanstalt.

Steinmetz, George. 1997. "German Exceptionalism and the Origins of Nazism." In Ian Kershaw and Moshe Lewin, eds., *Stalinism and Nazism: Dictatorships in Comparison*. Cambridge, England: Cambridge University Press.

Sternhell, Ze'ev. 1985. "Anthropologie et politique: Les Avatars du darwinisme social au tournant du siècle." In EHESS, ed., *L'Allemagne nazie et le génocide juif*. Hautes Etudes. Paris: Gallimard, Seuil.

———. 1989. "Le Concept de fascisme." In Ze'ev Sternhell, Mario Sznajder, and Maia Ashéri, *Naissance de l'idéologie fasciste*. Paris: Fayard.

———. 1997. *La Droite révolutionnaire (1885–1914): Les Origines françaises du fascisme*. Paris: Folio-Gallimard.

Steyn, Juliet. 1995. "Charles Dickens' *Oliver Twist:* Fagin as a Sign," and Bryan Cheyette, "Neither Black nor White: The figure of 'the Jew' in Imperialist British literature." In Linda Nochlin and Tamar Garb, eds., *The Jew in the Text: Modernity and the Construction of Identity*. London: Thames & Hudson.

Streit, Christian. 1991. "Ostkreig: Antibolschewismus und 'Endlösung.' " *Geschichte und Gesellschaft,* no. 17.


Taine, Hyppolite. 1902. *Hyppolite Taine: Sa vie et sa correspondance*. Vol. 4. Paris: Hachette.

————. 1972. *Les Origines de la France contemporaine: La Révolution, l'anarchie.* Paris: Laffont.

Taguieff, Pierre-André. 1992. *Les Protocoles des sages de Sion: Faux et usages d'un faux.* 2 vols. Paris: Berg International.

————. 1998. *La Couleur et le sang: Doctrines racistes à la française.* Paris: Mille et une nuits.

Talmon, Jacob L. 1952. *The Origins of Totalitarian Democracy.* London: Secker & Warburg.

Tarde, Gabriel. 1892. "Les Crimes des foules." *Archives de l'anthropologie criminelle,* no. 7.

Taylor, Frederick W. 1977. "The Principles of Scientific Management." 1911. In *Scientific Management.* Westport, Conn.: Greenwood Press.

Theweleit, Klaus. 1978. *Männerphantasien.* 2 vols. Frankfurt: Verlag Roter Stern.

Tocqueville, Alexis de. 1961. *De la démocratie en Amérique.* 4 vols. 1835–40. Reprint, Paris: Folio-Gallimard.

————. 1967, *L'Ancien Régime et la Révolution.* 1856. Reprint, Paris: Folio-Gallimard.

————. 1986. *Souvenirs.* Paris: Laffont.

————. 1991. "Travail sur l'Algérie." 1841. In *Oeuvres.* Paris: Pléiade-Gallimard.

Tombs, Robert. 1997. *La Guerre contre Paris 1871.* Paris: Aubier.

Tranfaglia, Nicola. 1995. *Dalla prima Guerra mondiale al fascismo.* Turin: UTET.

Traverso, Enzo. 1992. *Les Juifs et l'Allemagne: De la "symbiose judéo-allemande" à la mémoire d'Auschwitz.* Paris: La Découverte.

————. 1997a. *L'Histoire déchirée: Essai sur Auschwitz et les intellectuals.* Paris: Les Editions du Cerf.

————. 1997b. "La Shoah, les historiens et l'usage public de l'histoire: A propos de l'affaire Daniel J. Goldhagen." *L'Homme et la Société* 3, no. 125.

————. 1997c. *Les Marxistes et la question juive: Histoire d'un débat 1843–1943.* Paris: Kimé.

————. 1999. "La Singularité d'Auschwitz: Problèmes et dérives de la recherché historique." In Catherine Coquio, ed., *Parler des camps, penser les génocides.* Paris: Albin Michel.

————. 2001. Introduction to Traverso, ed., *Le Totalitarisme: Le vingtième Siècle en débat.* Paris: Seuil.

Tuck, Richard. 1999. *The Right of War and Peace: Political Thought and the International Order from Grotius to Kant.* Oxford: Clarendon Press.

Turner, Frederick Jackson. 1986. "The Significance of the Frontier in American History." 1893. Reprinted in *The Frontier in American History* (Tucson: University of Arizona Press).

Ubershär, Gerd R., and Wolfram Wette. 1984. *"Unternehmen Barbarossa": Der deutsche Überfall auf die Sowjetunion, 1941—Berichte, Analysen, Dokumente.* Paderborn: Egon Verlag.

Vacher de Lapouge, Georges. 1896. *Les Sélections sociales: Cours libre de science politique professé à l'université de Montpellier (1888–1889).* Paris: Fontemoing.

————. 1909. "Observations sur l'infériorité naturelle des classes pauvres." In *Race et milieu social: Essais d'anthroposociologie*. Paris: Marcel Rivière.

Van Oosterzee, Penny. 1997. *When Worlds Collide: The Wallace Line*. Ithaca, N.Y.: Cornell University Press.

Venturi, Franco. 1970. *Utopia e riforma nell'illuminismo*. Turin: Einaudi.

Vialles, Noélie. 1987. *Le Sang et la chair: Les Abattoirs des pays d'Adour*. Paris: Editions de la Maison des Sciences de l'Homme.

Vidal-Naquet, Pierre. 1991. *Les Juifs, la mémoire et le present*. Vol. 2. Paris: La Découverte.

Villa, Renzo. 1985. *Il deviante e i suoi segni: Lombroso e la nascita dell'antropologia criminale*. Milan: Angeli.

Wallace, Alfred Russel. 1864. "The Origins of Human Races and the Antiquity of Man Deduced from the Theory of 'Natural Selection.' " *Journal of the Anthropological Society*.

————. 1891. "Natural Selection." 1870. In *Natural Selection and Tropical Nature: Essays on Descriptive and Theoretical Biology*. London: Macmillan.

Walser Smith, Helmut. 1998. "The Talk of Genocide: The Rhetoric of Miscegenation—Notes on the Debates in the German Reichstag Concerning South-West Africa 1904–1914." In Sara Friedrichsmayer, Sara Lennox, and Susanne Zantop, eds., *The Imperialist Imagination: German Colonialism and Its Legacy*. Ann Arbor: University of Michigan Press.

Walzer, Michael, ed. 1989. *Régicide et révolution: Le Procès de Louis XVI*. Paris: Payot. Translation of *Regicide and Revolution: Speeches on the Trial of Louis XVI* (Cambridge: Cambridge University Press, 1974).

Warmbold, Joachim. 1989. *Germania in Africa: Germany's Colonial Literature*. Frankfurt: Peter Lang.

Weber, Max. 1956. *Wirtschaft und Gesellschaft*. 2 vols. 1922. Reprint, Jübingen: J. C. B. Mohr.

————. 1988. "Parlement und Regierung im neugeordneten Deutschland." In *Gesammelte politische Schriften*. 1921. Reprint, Tübingen: J. C. B. Mohr.

————. 1978. *Economy and Society*. 1922. English translation, Berkeley, Los Angeles, and London: University of California Press.

Webster, Nesta. 1921. *World Revolution*. London: Constable.

Wehler, Hans-Ulrich. 1985. *The German Empire 1871–1918*. London: Berg Publishers.

Weindling, Paul. 1998. *Health, Race and German Politics Between National Unification and Nazism, 1870–1947*. 2 vols. Cambridge, England: Cambridge University Press.

Wesseling, H. L. 1989. "Colonial Wars: An Introduction." In J. A. de Moor and H. L. Wesseling, eds., *Colonialism and War: Essays on Colonial Wars in Asia and Africa*. Leiden: E. J. Brill/Universitaire Pers Leiden.

Weidemann, Hans-Rudolf. 1992. "Ein schönes Schneiden!" Ein unbekannter Brief Soemmerings über die Guillotine." *Medizinhistorisches Journal* 27, nos. 1–2.

Wieviorka, Annette. 1977. "L'Expression 'camp de concentration." *Vingtième Siècle*, no. 54.

Winock, Michel. 1982. "Edouard Drumont et *La France juive.*" In *Nationalisme, an-tisémitisme et fascisme en France.* Paris: Seuil.

Winter, Jay. 2000. "Shell-Shock." *Journal of Contemporary History* 35, no. 1, special issue.

Wippermann, Wolfgang. 1981. *Der "Deutsche Drang nach Osten": Ideologie und Wirklichkeit eines politischen Schlagwortes.* Darmstadt: Wissenschaftliche Buchge-sellschaft.

Wismann, Cornelia. 1977. "Starting from Scratch: Concepts of Order in No Man's Land." In Bernd Hüppauf, ed., *War, Violence and the Modern Condition.* Berlin: Walter de Gruyter.

Wistrich, Robert. 1997. "Hitler et ses aides." *Le Débat,* no 93.

Yerushalmi, Yosef Hayim. 1998. "Assimilation et antisémitisme racial: Le Modèle ibérique et le modèle allemand." *Sefardica: Essais sur l'histoire des juifs, des marranes et des nouveaux chrétiens d'origine hispano-portugaise.* Paris: Chandeigne.

Zola, Emile. 1972. *The Debacle.* Harmondsworth: Penguin Classics.

# INDEX